Your Hero and Mine, Scott

To Pat,

On behalf of
my brother, Scott

Clyde R Christopher

Christofferson Enterprises LC

Copyright 2008 by Christofferson Enterprises LC

Written by Scott A. Christofferson
Designed by Carrie Handy
Edited by Carrie Handy and Kit Lammert

For information about discounts for bulk purchases, please go to
www.yourheroandmine.com

ISBN 13: 978-0-9817978-0-9
ISBN 10: 0-9817978-0-6

YOUR HERO
AND MINE,
Scott

By Scott Andrew Christofferson

With Foreward and Epilogue
by
Carrie Christofferson Handy

Dedication

This collection of letters chronicling Scott's journey into adulthood and his death on a battlefield in Vietnam, is dedicated to our mother, Barbara Jerome Christofferson Hurd, and to the memory of our father, the late Frank E. Christofferson, on behalf of our brother, Scott.

> Clyde R Christofferson
> Jan E. Christofferson Ferland
> James F. Christofferson
> Carrie J. Christofferson Handy
> Kit F. Christofferson Lammert
> Carl L. Christofferson
> Frank C. Christofferson

Above: a rare photo of all eight Christofferson children, with their mother, Barbara circa 1961; from left: Kit, Clyde, Scott, Barbara ,Carl, Frank (baby), Jan; lower front right: Carrie, Jim

Acknowledgments

While the letters that comprise the bulk of this book are the work of our brother, Scott Christofferson, many of his words would have been lost if not for the kindness of those who shared with us their personal correspondence from Scott after his death. Because of their generosity, we were able to piece together a more complete picture of Scott and of his experiences from the time of his high school graduation in the Spring of 1965 to his death in Vietnam in October of 1967. In addition to the many letters to our immediate family that comprise the bulk of this book, we were able to include a few other key letters that have helped round out Scott's story. We would like to thank James Gordon (J.G.) Carnachan, (now deceased), attorney, family friend and faithful correspondent of Scott's, and Ted Myrick and John Stann, high school classmates and close friends of Scott's; for passing along his letters and in so doing, sharing the Scott they knew with us.

Scott in his paratrooper gear, circa Spring 1966

CONTENTS

When I leave this tortured land,

In some more peaceful place I'll stand,

I'll raise my arms and lift my voice,

"Know something funny? I had no choice."

YOUR HERO AND MINE, *Scott*

Foreward

The autumn of 1967, for me, was filled with the drama and trivialities of being in the Sixth Grade. If a world existed outside of my orbit, I'm not sure I noticed until the day the Western Union man appeared at our door with a telegram announcing the news that Scott was Missing in Action near Chu Lai, Vietnam. Even then, the grim reality did not register in my 11 year old brain in the same way it no doubt did for my parents and my older siblings. I remember thinking, "Oh dear! He's lost! I hope they find him soon."

I recall arriving home from school a day or so later with my siblings and being met by our mother, her uncharacteristically red-rimmed eyes telling the story before she opened her mouth. I had sat down at the piano to play a favorite piece; the music stopped when I saw her face. Scott was dead.

Ironically, his smiling face had appeared in a group photo in the St. Louis Post Dispatch on the very day he died, part of a public relations piece he helped put together, which featured soldiers who were St. Louis Cardinals fans posing with a banner highlighting their high hopes for a Cardinals World Series win that year.

Scott's death on October 8 of 1967 was a defining event for the Christofferson family. For me and the other "younger" kids, it was a dubious mark of honor to have lost a sibling in Vietnam, but we didn't really know the brother who at 19 had given his life in a war halfway around the world. It wasn't until some fifteen years later, when I discovered a box of his letters stored in a closet at my mother's home in Arkansas, that I at last got to know Scott. As I read the letters, I came to recognize his humor and wit and to know his intensity and idealism. His letters tell his story in a way that not only let him back into my life, but helped me understand what took him to Vietnam, and what he left there.

My siblings and I believe others will be able to gain insight into that period in American history by reading these letters, to develop an appreciation for the young men and women who sacrificed their youth in the jungles of Vietnam, and perhaps most significantly, to know well one specific young man whose journey from college dropout to Army combat reporter to fallen hero is brought to vivid life through his own words. For that reason, and because it was Scott's fervent desire to be a writer, we have chosen to share his letters in this book.

To have worked on this project with my 6 siblings has been an unexpected blessing in the tragedy of losing our brother. I thank them for allowing me the indulgence of inserting myself into Scott's book by writing this foreward as well as an epilogue to his story.

A final note: I have edited Scott's letters minimally for clarity and spelling, leaving in idiomatic spellings ("thot") and expressions as much as possible. I have added a few footnotes when I felt it necessary to understand his references. All poetry included is Scott's original work, found in his journal writings.

Carrie Christofferson Handy

At Scott's urging, his parents bought him a one-way ticket to Alaska following his high school graduation in 1965, so he could spend the summer before entering college pursuing Alaskan adventure and a paying job. Above, he is accompanied to the airport by his family, including (from left) little brother Carl, Dad, older brother Clyde, and sisters Kit and Carrie.

14

Chapter I.
British Columbia

7/24/65

Dear Mr. Carnachan,

I finally got those clippings you sent me a month ago. I appreciate them and can really use them where I am because reading material is a bit scarce.

I hear there is a mail strike going on here, so I don't know when you'll get this letter (I think 1st class will get thru).

In case you don't know what's happened to me, I'll fill you in.

On June 17, I began a 2-day flight to Anchorage, Alaska in search of fame, fortune and dinero. Had I arrived 2 weeks earlier, I would now probably be working for $30 a day skimming seal somewhere in the Arctic Ocean. But alas! I was 2 weeks late, and because of a crush of out-of-staters seeking work, I couldn't find a job of any kind. The price for room and board in Anchorage is outrageous, and I couldn't afford to stay there any longer, so after 2 futile days looking for work I hitch-hiked out. In the Matanuska Farm Valley I could have got a job—if I waited around for about 2 weeks. I hitched into the Yukon and down across the border to Haines, Alaska. No work. I went back up and then to Whitehorse—no work. I crossed the border into British Columbia and was intending to go to California (the land of milk and honey) when I got a ride with a fellow who happened to be a personnel manager of a large Canadian firm. He offered me a job and I took it.

Now I am working at an oil camp 100 miles north of Dawson Creek, British Columbia. Because I am a

U.S. citizen without a work permit, the only kind of job I can hold in Canada is a casual labor job. I am a lowly Camp Attendant, which is really a floor scrubber, sheet changer and washer, toilet cleaner, etc. etc. The pay is low and the hours long (56 hrs./week) but it's okay because I have met a lot of great people and am out on my own.

I don't know if it's simply a rebellion, emotion or whatever, but I am no longer a Catholic. Not only that, but I have actually *gasp* condemned all (all) religions. It is really very odd. I am very strongly anti-church, and have very weak arguments to support myself. The fact that my arguments are weak does not phase me in the least, because, doggonit, I'll invent reasons if I have to, to be away from the influence of religion. I guess I have great faith (the kind of faith that moves mountains?) in my anti-religion philosophy. Well, here it is: the way I see it, man wasn't intended to be a sheep, to be led in his beliefs and faith. (I know this is weak, but it gets stronger.) The way I see it, the purpose of man being here (assuming there *is* a purpose), is destroyed if man is led and does not think things out for himself and decide how he wants to do things. I have seen too many people who follow a faith merely because of tradition or custom. So I don't think god (assuming there is one, and he has an ulti- mate purpose for us) would have used churches. *gasp* And not only am I anti-church, but I am also anti-Christ, along with Nietzsche. I have, in my quest for my own philosophy, eliminated the Golden Rule. "Do unto others as you would have them do unto you." Fine. But what if "you" are a masochist or a pervert? I think a more definite philosophy is needed. I have been doing a lot of thinking on the subject, serious thinking, and have come up with this: Don't hurt anyone needlessly or purposely. To me, with a lot of thot behind it, this means quite a bit. (Don't tell my mom about this because I'm afraid if she knew, she'd have a heart attack and die.) I'm not narrow minded enough to condemn the people in Church, because if the

Church satisfies their needs, that's their business. All I'm saying is Churches (I have looked into quite a few and decided they were basically all alike) are no good for me. I have read Hugh Hefner's (of Playboy) "Playboy Philosophy" and I agree with some of the stuff he says. The "Philosophy" seems to be a serious attempt to examine our life, not just a rationalization for sex.

Other news:

Item: My girlfriend (big true-love romance) has written me a mere 88 words so far, and pretty soon I'll give her up for lost—unless she writes me a big letter pretty quick. I've had a couple of romances before this one, but this one seems to be "it." We both communicate with each other on a variety of subjects (philosophy included). Rather, we did communicate on a variety of subjects before I left. But it seems destined for oblivion anyhow, because we'll be going to different colleges. I'm sure she will get very impressed by some upperclassman. I'm also sure I'll fall prey to some worthy freshwoman. I guess I'm a masochist because I have been prolonging it throughout this summer anyway. (I even envision a triumphant return from these Canadian wilds.) But like I say, I guess it was doomed anyway. That's the way it goes.

Item: I have had my first encounter with a large quantity of booze. It was quite exhilarating and I suffered no after effects. (Except frequent urination. Beer seems to run right thru.)

Item: I have decided on the Army ROTC program (rather than the Navy-Marine) because I don't relish dying in a place like the Dominican Republic or Panama, about which I couldn't care less. The way I figure it, if the U.S. gets involved in a war big enough to put the Army into action, I will want to be in it anyway. But I don't want to get killed because of the "big stick."

Item: I have decided to enter pre-journalism this year. Don't tell my parents this because they have threatened to kill me if I start majoring in my first year. They don't seem to realize that the program is flexible enough so that I can change at almost any time with little difficulty.

Item: After I graduate I plan to start a magazine. I have been thinking in detail about this for several years and I have come up with some good ideas. Good ideas both for the magazine's format and content, and also for its promotion. I have some novel ideas and I think they can succeed.

How is Mrs. Carnachan? I really enjoyed seeing and talking with her. She plays a vicious, fast game of chess.

A book I read recently that you might like: *The Natural* by Bernard Malamud. It is an excellent novel.

Alaska is quite a place. Mountainous, rugged, green, lots of streams and lakes. Any running stream is safe to drink from. The people I met there were individualistic, independent and friendly. The only real fools I met were in Anchorage. Cities seem to corrupt people. Canada is also quite a place. People are scarce (only 18 million) and a town of 4000 is considered big. The country is beautiful. After I make my first million (if things go as planned, I should be 25 or so at the time), I am going to expatriate and homestead a section (640 acres) of land in Canada.

It's an interesting experience.

Sincerely,

Scott A. Christofferson

7/24/65
SA Christofferson
Kenyon's Rig #12
Ft. St. John, B.C.
Canada

Ted,

Just thot I'd write to you so you know what happened to me. I spent 2 days in Anchorage looking for work. It seems I came at the wrong time (2 weeks earlier they were hiring anyone available) so I couldn't find a job. There must have been a million out of staters looking for work. Prices were outrageous. I hitch-hiked out toward the Matanuska Farm Valley. I could have gotten a job there if I waited around for 2 weeks but nuts to that so I kept going. I went thru the Yukon and south to the Alaskan border on into Haines. No work there. That night the 2 guys I was hitching a ride with got me drunk on my ass. I didn't suffer any after effects except very frequent urination. Beer seems to run right thru.

Next day I went back up to the Yukon to Whitehorse. We got there late at night and boy was that town wild. Booze was everywhere. What an opportunity. But I was in a very moral mood at the time so I stayed in the car while the driver went out and got shocked up.

Couple days later I got to Dawson Creek. I decided to go to California (the land of milk and honey) and the first ride I got the driver offered me a job. I took it and am now working in an oil camp 100 miles north of Dawson Creek, in the middle of nowhere.

The country north is beautiful. The people are independent, individualistic, and out of their minds. The guys in the camp go into town (Ft. St. John is closest) once a week and get shit-faced and shocked up with a squaw. A couple have never come back and are presumed either still shocked up or in jail. I work a 56 hour week. But the pay is so shit that I'll only come out a couple hundred ahead. However, I think the experience is well worth it.

I've really changed. I've decided to become a Bohemian after college for a couple of years. I've lost my religion and live by this creed: Never do anything that will hurt anyone needlessly or purposely. Once in a while I get pretty high with the others. In short, I've totally lost my mind—but I'll be OK (but changed) once I get back.

How're things going with Lee Ann? I've written Penny lots but all she's written me so far is a short 1 page note. I'm afraid she has decided to end it, but I'm still hoping.

Did you find a job? What do you plan to do next summer? I think I'll either work (thru some students at Mizzou in the South or voter registrations), (sic) or go somewhere like this summer.

I've decided to take Army ROTC. I don't especially want to be in a place like Panama or the Dominican Republic. I figure if the Army ever gets involved, it will be a pretty serious war and I'll want to be in it anyhow.

If Penny hasn't ditched me totally by Sept., I'm going to take her out and spend about $50 on her. I like her an awful lot.

I don't get too much U.S. news here. One of the fellows told me something about riots in Missouri on the 4th. Anybody I know?

I bought a guitar. It's pretty cheap but I think it's OK.

Around here I've seen bear, caribou, hawks, ravens, and vultures. Down around Haines I saw moose (no horns this time of year, and they sort of looked like mules) and bear. I could shoot myself because I had only 1 roll of film when I was in Alaska. Write me if you can.

Scott

Chapter II.
Mizzou

9/11/65

Dear everyone,

Got your letters, Kit, Carrie and Mom.
Room looked like heck when I got here. Since, I painted it, so it looks livable now. We could use a rug. If you have any old curtains around, please send them. The window is about 6' high and 5' wide. Match with blue walls.

Orientation was basically a drag.
Got my account transferred.
Have $8 cash. $347.09 in bank.

Big expenses—

$10—season football tickets
$143.75—incidental fees, ROTC uniform deposit, etc.
$45.35—books
$7.50—yearbook

Work—Wednesday and Sat. nites, help clean up after dinner. Caught some poison ivy doing yard work last Sun.

Classes—Phys.ed., Monday and Wed.
ROTC, Tues., Thurs.
Spanish, daily
Math (college algebra), M, W, F
Western Civ.—Tues., Thurs., Sat.
English Masterpieces—Tues., Thurs.,

Classes start Monday Have 25 hr. work/study plan. Wish me luck.

Nice campus. Doing ok.

Scott

9/20/65

Hello everyone—

Economic front-
The way I figure it, $64 in mid January should carry me for the semester. Being a month shorter, next semester should cost a hundred dollars less than this one. Also, I'll get 50% back on my books in January. Altogether, this year should cost about $1,100. Barring anything unexpected, the $64 in Jan..will suffice for this semester.

Please send up some curtains with Jan this Sat. We can really use them.

Social front—
Last Sat. the Tigers lost to Kentucky, 7-0. A poor defensive secondary and a weak attack, plus 4 fumbles and 3 interceptions, cost us the game.

I haven't met any fantastic co-eds yet. This is not to say that there aren't any. I just haven't met them yet.

This Friday I've got a blind date from Christians. She's supposed to be 5'5", brunette and good looking....I hope so.

Last Sunday I went on a Newman picnic. I really can't say much for the girls I saw there. The good looking ones they had at the Newman introductory dance must have been hired as a come on. Actually, the picnic was fine until it started raining. Man, did it pour! Everyone got soaked.

I got elected Athletic Chairman for the house. I like it here. Out of the 25 or so games of chess I've played so far, I've only lost 5.

Every Sunday night the school shows free flicks. I've seen "The List of Adrian Messenger" and "On the Waterfront." Next week they have "Bigot" and later on, "The L-Shaped Room."

I read <u>Lisa and David</u> and <u>Jack</u>. Great books.

This Sat. is a mixer with Stephens. I'll be going to it.

Educational front—

I've been studying pretty much. I have 5 hours a day scheduled but have yet to use them all. But I imagine things will pick up shortly.

English Masterpieces is great. A wonderful class. A real morale builder. The girls are fabulous. The course is okay, too. This ½ semester is for short stories; the other half for poetry.

Spanish is going okay. I should do well.

College Algebra is slow. The teacher (young lady) spends too much time on simple stuff. I wish she'd speed up.

Western Civ is cool. The lecturer is terrific. He's the best speaker I've heard.

P.E. is terrible. I've got Orientation in Opposition to Fitness and we sit around watching movies. Real bad.

I dropped ROTC. Since it became non-compulsory this year, its enrollees are dedicated and very gung-ho. ¾ of them are on scholarship. There is a quota and I doubt if I could make it. My schedule is much freer without it. I couldn't stand it.

When I graduate from here, or leave it otherwise, I will enlist in either the Army or the Marines for my service.

As far as I can see, my grades should be okay.

Miscellaneous front—

I saw Becky the other day.

I haven't heard from Ray yet. He's going to Ark. A&M. Next semester I think I'll get a part time job. Just a couple days a week.

I've liked the cards you sent me, Mom. Your humor keeps me going. Crazy, that is. Not really, I just wish you'd send more, not to get sickening or anything, but it's just good to find some mail.

I guess I'll be seeing Jan this weekend.

I hope Dad and Clyde are having fun in the basement. I can't wait to see it done.

Sounds like the little kids are doing okay in school. They must be quite the thing at Price. Five in one school.

The campus is great and once you get to know it, it's lots of fun.

When Jan comes up, send Carnachan's book with her. I still haven't written him.

Everyone write me.

Scott

1/20/66

Hi!—Just a short note:

Well, I'm ¾ way thru finals. My last one is Monday afternoon.

It was great to get those letters. And the check. I really needed it. Too bad you couldn't make the bash in Denver. It probably would have been fun.

Not much has been happening around here. I've been dating a girl named Sally. Been to some parties. Contemplating deep thots. My latest kick is deism—the impersonal god bit. Mizzou's basketball team stinks. Am reading <u>Zorba the Greek</u>. Say—see "the Pawnbroker:" a great flick. Read <u>Tortilla Flat</u> in the Steinbeck book I got for Xmas. Real good and very deep.

Can't think of much else to say.

See you.

Scott

FINANCIAL REPORT   Oct. 25, 1965

Ammount started out with : $ 546.19
Cash on Hand   : 159.27
Expendetures this far   : 386.92

Check # / amnt / what		Break down	
1	$10.00	Football ticket	Room + Board $114.50
2	193.75	Fees	Spending $ 28.00
3	45.35	Books	records, tickets
			Record player, shoes, 47.52
4	53.00	Co-op	School expenses 197.10
5	10.00	Me	$ 386.92
6	24.60	Record player	
7	12.00	Me	
8	61.50	Co-op	Room + Board for Nov. + Dec will be about
9	6.00	Me	$62.00 apiece : $124.00 Projected
10	8.00	Ticket home	miscleanas expenses will be about $40:
11	4.49	Record club	$164.00. I'll need some money in Late
12	8.25	Shoes	December. In January (should I live so
$ 386.92			long) I'll need money for books, + fees (near

$200.) The entire year should be around
$1,200.

                Scott

Jan. 24, 1966

Dear Mom and Dad:

Since I'll have to serve three years in the service anyway, and right now I can't get too excited about college; I've enlisted. Because I want something challenging I volunteered for the Army Airborne. Boot camp and jump school will be at Ft. Benning, Ga. After boot camp, 6 weeks, I'll have a 14 day leave, during which I'll bring my stuff home from the Co-op and, if I'm not totally disowned, spend some time at home.

Sorry I did it this way, but I figured it would be better than having a big fight about it—during which I would probably have been killed or disinherited. But I see no reason for us not to get along.

Now: the reason. The only purpose I would have right now to get a degree would be for a high paying job. Right now I can't think of any job like that that I would want to have. All I want to do is be a writer. No college can teach me that, so why should I go. If I should decide to go to college after the Army, I could do so on loan. Or if I could make $1200 in the summer, I could do it by myself. But that would be after the Army. Right now I can't see it.

Here are the reasons people go to college:

To get a degree necessary for the job they want.
(A good reason, but it doesn't apply to me.)

To please their parents. (You're not that type and neither am I.)

To avoid the draft. (No fooling, this is a <u>major</u> reason.)

Because they're too stupid to think of anything else to do. (Not me)

To get married. (Not me.)

To pursue higher thot. (Unfortunately, this isn't done very well in the classroom.)

So, if and when I find a reason to go to college, I will do so. Until then, I will do what I think more important. At the risk of sounding like a typical teenager, but because my sentiments are identical, I will quote two lines from a current hit song by the Animals: "It's my life and I'll do what I want. It's my mind and I'll think what I want, show me I'm wrong."

By the time you get this letter, I'll be in Georgia. I will send you my address as soon as I find out what it will be. Don't worry about me, and although you probably think I'm wrong, please wish me luck.

Love, Scott

Scott in an undated photo, circa 1965

Chapter III.
Fort Leonard Wood

27 Jan 66

Please put this civilian clothing somewhere. In case this beats home a letter I'll write tomorrow --expect a letter real soon.

I'll send you an address as soon as we get sent for basic training. I have a letter of guarantee for the Airborne, so after basic I'll have a 14 day leave, then I'll go to Ft. Benning, GA. for jump school. Basic will be in Leonard Wood, tho. It will be 8 or 9 weeks starting the 4th of February. I hope you got the postcard I sent the night I got here.

Having a swell time.

Love, Scott

p.s. Also find letter dated 24th inside.

Sat. –'29 '66 (January)

Hello everyone –

Just got off the phone from talking to you. Was great to hear you.

Too bad Harvard turned Clyde down. I can't see why they did.

Briefly, I'll tell you what's happened. 14 Mon. night – left by bus for St. Louis – the Army generously paid my bus fare. That nite I spent in the U.S. enlistment place at 12th and Spruce. They have a barracks there for guys taking physicals. They got us up at 5 Tuesday and we ate. We started testing at 7:00 and continued thru 11:30. Then I took the physical and came thru real good. "A" physique rating. A really touching scene there: Now, most of those guys taking physicals were draftees and some of them not particularly anxious to be physically qualified. This one guy, with tears in his eyes, was turned down as 12 lbs. overweight. He really wanted to get in and he couldn't, when all those other guys were begging to be exempted, and crying that they <u>weren't</u> exempted.

I got my letter of guarantee after passing the physical. I had to show the results of my mentals and physical to this army guy to see if I was qualified enough. My mentals were considerably higher than average and my physical real good. At 3:10 we were sworn in. We ate and left by bus for F.L.W. at 5:30. We got here at 8:30 and were briefed and issued bedding and put in barracks. Wednesday we were issued clothing. 4 fatigue shirts and pants, 2 pr. boots, 4 pair wool socks, 2 summer hats, 1 winter hat, 1 field jacket, 2 belts, 1 chess hat, 2 winter chess shirts, 1 chess jacket, pants, etc. etc. etc. etc. A full duffel bag and some. We got haircuts and did the other stuff. Thursday we took more tests. Friday we took more tests and had several briefings. Today we just sat around. We were scheduled to have penicillin shots – but nothing. So, you are up to date.

Every night we have to have five guards. 1 man walks for an hour on both floors looking for fires. Crazy: we go to bed at 9 (lights off then, but talking and messing around for a while) and get up at 4:45. Lights go on again at 5 and we have to fall in for chow at 5:15.

Dad—please note the enclosed picture.

Scott

Scott A. Christofferson RA 17729663
Leadership School
Class LOC Class #3166
Ft. Leonard Wood, Mo. 65475

All that is my address. Mail letters airmail before Wednesday-9th or I won't get it. We'll get assigned Friday night after graduation ceremonies. "Zero week," a week of general preparing and messing around before basic, will be from Fri. until Mon. the 21st. Then basic starts. So that puts my leave back to about the 18th of April. If I graduate, and I feel I will, I will wear either corporal or sergeant's stripes on the band on my arm. It won't make me that rank, of course, but it will make me a platoon leader. I will get some privileges along with the extra work: like giving out passes. And you know who will get the first weekend pass. Most likely it won't come until after 5 weeks of basic because of cases of URI (upper respiratory infection) —but I will almost positively be able to get home before the end of basic. There are 60 of us in the LOC class (not LOS as I put before on the other post-card) and about 59 or 60 should pass. The army needs LOC's pretty bad, so the flunk out rate is very small. The only way they flunk you is over your attitude. If I want to go to OCS I can do so any time after Airborne. It involves a 23-week course in Kentucky and makes me a 2nd Lt., but I don't know if I want it. According to local 2nd Lts., enlisted like me, it is a lot of trouble and a bad job. Everyone please write and send it airmail.

Scott

Fort Leonard Wood

9 Feb. 66

Pvt. Scott A Christofferson
RA 17729663
Company B 4ᵗʰ Battalion 2ⁿᵈ BCT
Ft. Leonard Wood, Mo. 65475

Hello everyone—

I decided to PRINT big this letter so as you all could read it without too much trouble.

The LOC program is a leadership orientation course to provide assistant platoon leaders and squad leaders. I have two more days until I graduate, although I came within a hair's of being thrown out of LOC completely along with 9 other LOC's. Briefly, we were caught by our sergeant at the PX without permission. I won't come out and say what we were doing there, but if you're 18 you <u>can</u> buy beer at a post PX.....however, Sergeant Miller is a very understanding man and he let us off with a few days of KP. It was really a wild scene, all the LOC's scrambled for the back door when he came in, but the back door was barred shut, so we hit the dirt in an attempt to avoid detection. He just walked past us like he didn't see us, but we were in for a surprise when we got back to the barracks. The next morning at inspection he made us all recite the General Orders and he really looked for mistakes in our beds, foot lockers and wall lockers. All he found wrong with mine was I didn't button few shirts.

This course has been fun. Bayonet training, hand to hand combat, M-14 assembly and disassembly, physical training, lectures and lots else. We're cramming an awful lot into this week. We'll have a "0 week" from this Monday to Monday 21ˢᵗ. Basic will really start the 21ˢᵗ, 8 weeks from that is April 18ᵗʰ, but graduation will be the 15ᵗʰ. So I should be home then. On visitors: this is possible, depending on the commanding officer. During "0 week" on a Sunday it is very possible to have visitors. So, if you can come down this Sunday or next, let me know. I'd really like it.

I got a funny letter from Roger. I told him I was joining—and his letter was appropriate and hilarious.

Jim—being how the 26 and 27 is the weekend, it is possible that I could see you. Tell your scoutmaster the situation and ask him to find out approximately where you'll be here. This is a pretty huge place, so if we don't know where each other is, we'd never get together. I'll try to find out where they put Boy Scouts for these kinds of things, but write me and tell me what you find out. I really appreciated your letter. Wait till I get ahold of you! Ha! Ha! By the way, I made the same trip when I was in Boy Scouts. I guess that's what made me choose the Army. Another thot – as I'll be in only my 1st week of basic, it might be impossible for me to gain post liberty, which I would need to go somewhere else on the Post to see you.

Carrie—thanks for the letter. Sounds like you're doing good in school—keep it up!

Kit—thanks for your picture. I showed it to all the guys here and they think it's great.

Carl—As they're other guys here going into the paratroopers like myself, your picture of men jumping from planes went over real big. I hear you can read real good now. Send me a letter sometime and tell me what you're doing.

Frank—Good to hear from you. Send me more pictures—I really enjoy them.

Jan—let me know of your plans for M.U. Maybe, if you're awful slow, and don't get married, I'll get to go there at the same time you will. I won't have any trouble getting back into 3-Squares so that's where I'll live. Having a ball. (Send me a letter, and I'll write you one soon too.)

From mom's letter I understand that dad got a

big kick out of that crazy postcard. I knew you would
when I filled it out. It was really good to talk to you over
the phone and I hope maybe you and some of the family
could come down here some Sunday. Because I'll be either
an assistant platoon sergeant or a squad leader in Basic I
know I could get post liberty later on, but for the first few
Sundays all I could possibly get is maybe a half hour on
Sunday in the Company area only. Even this is doubt-
ful—tho some people I know have had visitors---because
of an attempt to quarantine U.R.I. (upper respiratory infection). However, this depends on the conditions of
U.R.I. at that time. I had my hair cut again—<u>2
TIMES***IN 2 WEEKS!!!!!!!!!**</u> (wow! gosh!)

     Thanks a lot for the letter mom. I'm glad you're
keeping me posted, and I like your witticisms.

     Brief sketch of life in the Army—

     At 4:30 we all get up, 5:00 lights go on, 5:20 we
form up for chow, 6:30 inspection; 7:30 we have physical
training. Today, because of the "PX Affair," we double
timed 2 miles to "sweat the beer out of all you duds." A
"dud" is anything you want it to be—anything deroga-
tory. From 8:30 to chow we have classes in stuff like
bayonet fighting, hand to hand combat, military justice,
etc., etc. and other courses on leadership. After chow to
supper we have more classes. After chow (about 4:30 p.m.
usually) we have details of some sort and a little time to
ourselves.

10 Thurs. 9:30 p.m.

     Lights are out but I'm in the latrine finishing this
letter anyhow. Just got back from a work detail. Tomorrow we all graduate, hopefully. Today we had a PT test—
I scored among the 5 or so highest. There are 60 here. I'll
put this in an envelope now to make sure it gets mailed.
P.S. My record club will start sending newsletters to home
soon. Until I write you again just open them and send me
the IBM card <u>quickly</u>—within 2 days or forget it.

                         Scott

PVT Scott A. Christofferson RA17729663
B Company, 4th Battalion, 2nd BCT, 3rd Platoon
Ft. Leonard Wood, Mo.
12 Feb. '66

Hello everyone—
    I <u>did</u> graduate. Diploma and everything. We got
all dressed up in our class A uniforms with brass and everything. Speeches and dedication. The works. Just like
high school. Sgt. Miller, we are now pretty good friends,
scared the heck out of me, tho. The diplomas were read
off alphabetically and then you got up and went to the
stage and got the diploma. Well, Sgt. Miller, just to scare
me, put the diploma near the bottom of the stack. He
nearly busted out laughing when I went up to the stage,
pale and sweating. He's a swell guy.
    Right after graduation, trucks took us and our
duffels to our companies. This morning we had a briefing
by the company commander. He is, by the way, a captain
with Paratrooper and Ranger badges. You have to be a
Paratrooper to apply for either Rangers or Special Forces.
The difference between the two is Rangers fight more and
Special Forces, in groups of 10, try to organize and train
forces. There are lots in Viet Nam.
    Anyhow, after the Company Commander spoke
to us, we met our platoon sergeants. Mine and Bob
Curley's is Sgt. Brewere. There are two LOC's to a platoon. There are 60 men to a platoon, 6 platoons to a company, and 5 companies to the 4th Battalion. Altogether
there are about 1400 men in the 4th Battalion. I am one
of the 60 Assistant Sergeants. There are 12 in every company and our job is pretty important. So we have lots of
advantages to go along with the responsibility. Like: a
private room with the other Asst. Sgt.; post passes nearly
every weekend; all privates have to call us "Sergeant:" a
special table in the chow hall; first claim on the weekend
passes. We can also smoke. (I am still a non-smoker and

have no plans to start.) And talk during chow whereas everyone else but non-commissioned sgts. and commissioned officers can't talk or smoke. Actually, we are almost like non-coms; with the exceptions of pay and additional privileges of the rank. We got our stripes today. They are a buck sgt.'s stripes on a blue arm band. This will only last 8 weeks, so I'm going to get the most out of it.

I shouldn't have much trouble in basic, as far as the training and graduation goes. At the end we have to score at least 300 of 500 to pass the P.R. test. I don't know if I told you in the last letter but I got 393 on it. Only 5 people were above me. The qualifications for Airborne are pretty easy. Only 22 push ups (I did 50, for 100 pts., the Maximum in the P.R. test. No one else had above 45.) 80 (in 2 minutes) knee benders. I did 64 in 1 minute in the P.T. test, 1 short of the maximum. And a couple other exercises I can't remember. I must also run the mile in at least 8 ½ minutes. Last year in school I ran it in 5:37 so, although my clothes and boots will add weight, I shouldn't have much trouble there. We won't have to wear our field gear, either, during the run, so I guess I won't have any trouble getting into the Airborne.

Right now I'm sitting on my bunk in the 2nd platoon barracks. All the LOC's are here because they want us to stay together until the troops arrive. 34th Platoon should come in Monday—so that's when work will really start. A while ago we went to the Bravo Company Day room. T.V. room, pool table, writing room, and Coke machines. The officers have been instilling into us a great company pride. This is a crucial factor in training; a strong unit pride and esprit de corps. This pride moves the trainees to work harder for individual and unit awards at the end of basic. Daily, for example, at 5:15 when reveille is called, all platoons will run out of the barracks shouting Bravo! Bravo! (stands for B company) A is Alpha, C is Charley, D is Delta and E is Echo. At a daily inspection, during which the order for going to chow is determined by individual neatness in each platoon, there is a series of cheers designed to strengthen morale. Sgt. Johnson, a big career Negro, who, frankly scares the heck out of me, is the Company Assistant Commander. He has talked to us quite a bit yesterday and today. He taught us all the songs we'll sing while marching, and other company idiosyncrasies.

Jim—I asked him about the weekend I'll need post liberty to see you and he said sure. However, I doubt if I'll be able to do anything Sat. because of training, but for Sunday find out when you'll leave for St. Louis and what you'll be doing that day.

I'm having a good time—got to go to chow now. Write

Scott

14 Feb '66

Ted—

Thot I'd write you and fill you in on what's happened to me so far.

My parents took it just like I thot they would.

Got sworn in, after lots of testing, physicals, etc. , at 3:10 p.m. Tuesday 26 Jan. At 5:00 we got on a bus for Ft. Leonard Wood. Spent a week 1/2 in the Reception station—getting shots, taking more tests. On Friday 4th I was sent to LOC school: Leadership Orientation Course. There are 60 acting sergeants in a Battalion (1400 men or so). I am in B company of the 4th Battalion, third platoon. 60 guys in a platoon, not counting the 2 acting sergeants. In the 3rd platoon me and a guy named Bob Curley are the acting Sgts. I get to wear an arm band

that has buck sgt's stripes on it. The pvts. got to call me
"Sgt." I get a bunch of privileges regular guys in Basic
don't get, like a special table in the mess hall, talking and
smoking privileges during chow; post liberty; first chance
on weekend passes. However, I get a lot of responsibility
too. What acting sgts. are, are guys who are go-betweens
from the Drill Instructors to the men. So we are responsible for a lot of shit and catch hell if we fuck up.

Anyhow, LOC school was a week long and Friday
11th right after graduation, we got sent to our platoon.
I almost didn't graduate on account of I almost got court
martialed. Me and 8 other guys left the barracks without
permission and went to the PX, well you only have to be
18 to drink and naturally we all got drunk. Sgt. Miller,
the head of LOC, happened to come into the PX. We
were all pretty high and ran for the back door, which unfortunately, was barred shut. It was funnier than hell.
We hit the dirt and crawled around on the floor between
people's legs so Sgt. Miller wouldn't see us.

Well, he did see us, but he acted like he didn't.
When we got back to the barracks he was waiting for us.
The only thing that saved us, I guess, is that me and a guy
called Culivier were so damn funny, Sgt. Miller was laughing like hell at us. So he told us how we reminded him of
himself in his youth—but not for 2 days, during which we
got KP and thot we'd get court martialed. But I graduated all right because Sgt. Miller is a great guy and didn't
do anything to us. Altho, Sgt. Miller did put my diploma
way down at the bottom of the alphabet just to scare me
during graduation.

All LOC was, was a briefer on the crap we'll do in
basic. Bayonet training, hand to hand combat, M-14 disassembly and assembly, military courtesy, some other shit,
and a lot of the fundamentals of leadership.

The way we got picked for LOC was by doing
good on tests and aptitudes. I also did plenty good
enough to qualify for OCS (Officer's Candidate School)

but I'll decide on that later.

Basic will start the 21st. Our troops haven't come into B company yet, only us Acting Sgts. Are here, but they should come in either today or tomorrow. Basic will be about 8 weeks long, after which I'll get a 14 day leave. After that I'll go to Advanced Infantry training for another 8 weeks. After that I'll go to Airborne school for 3 or 4 weeks. Then I get a 30 day leave. On my overseas assignment request I put Viet Nam; on my state side assignment request I put Georgia—but the way things look in Viet Nam, I have a pretty great chance that I'll be there in 6 months.

I'll be in the Airborne—probably as a light weapons infantry man.

I hope you're doing good in school Don't drink too much. Have fun. Say hi to Lee for me. Write me if you get a chance.

Scott

At left: A pen and ink portrait drawn by Scott, circa 1965

23 Feb. '66

Hi, all you free people out there:

Finished a long day today. Carried our M-14's
around with us with pack all day. Yesterday I had Co.
headquarters duty from 9:00 yesterday morning to 6:00
this morning. 21 straight hours. No sleep. 2 hrs. physical training today, 3 hours drill and other stuff that took
up the whole day. Now I have to direct the cleaning of
our barracks for the daily barrack inspection tomorrow.
Today we came in second in the Company. Pretty soon
I'll go to bed. I got a valentine's card from Carrie—the
only reminder of that day. The lady who predicted JFK's
death and is 98% accurate predicted a disaster at F.L.W.
the 14th. It was supposed to have killed 5,000 but it never
came. We all eagerly awaited it.

Last week I was in the hospital with URI. About
1,000 cases on post. Spent 4 ½ days there—luckily I did-
n't miss anything as basic didn't start till Monday.

Got a letter from Roger—remember him—and
John Stann today. Really perked me up.

Spent most of last nite in "deep" philosophical
discussion with several interesting Negro permanent party
soldiers. I had a great time—the best since I've been here.
Those guys had such interesting lives. Both were real cool
speakers, and I wish I had a tape recorder to have recorded
them. It was great.

Jim—hurry and tell me about this weekend—
altho I guess I wouldn't get a letter in time. I'll just call
up the post locater and find out where you'll be. I think
you're 489, or is it 389? Who cares. If you're down here,
I'll find you Sunday. It'll be good to see someone from the
fambly.

If you have a free Sunday in a few weeks, come up
and bring the fambly. Write and let me know when or if
you'd come down so I can make plans. It would really be

swell to see some or all of you.

 With the new G.I. bill that recently got passed, it shouldn't be too much trouble economically when I go back to school.

 Well, my 40 hours with no sleep is catching... caught up with me and I am dead tired. So I'll sign off.

Scott

P.S. Write
P.P.S. I'll write again soon. It'll be a better letter

Pvt. Scott A Christofferson RA17729663
B-4-2
Ft. Leonard Wood, Mo

6 Mar. '66

Hi everyone—

 Got paid Friday! 67 dollars. As soon as I can I'll get to the post office and buy a money order to send to my bank account.

 Jan—I really appreciated the letter and cookies. So did the platoon. They were really good, and the platoon thanks you for them. Write me and tell me what Len's last name is so I can look him up. Let me know when you plan to come here. Just make sure it's a Sunday.

 I'm 2 weeks thru basic. I went to the OCS orientation pretty open minded but it didn't impress me much. Also, the idea of losing my guarantee made me decide not to sign now, altho because anytime during my time in the Army I can apply for OCS, I can still do it.

 Mom—there's a guy here in my platoon named Prickett. He's from Waverly, MN and knows the priest O'Flanagan.

 Dad—should I have claimed myself as an exemption? I wasn't sure what to do at the time, but it seemed like a good idea so I did.

Has Columbia Record sent anything to me at your address yet? If they do, it's probably an IBM order card. Please forward the letter quickly because if I don't take care of it before a certain date, they'll try and send me a record I don't want. Also please forward anything that 3-Squares forwarded to you.

If for an emergency you must get ahold of me, notify the St. Louis Red Cross and they'll get me quickly. If it isn't a big emergency and you want to get me, just call the FLW operator and ask for B 4 2/B company, 4th Battalion, 2nd BCT. This will get you the orderly room just outside my barracks and they'll send a runner for me. But don't do it unless it's something important.

9 Mar 66

Got your letters. Mom, you forgot the 2nd Bde. on the one you mailed the 21st so it was late. So there I was, reading it after mail call, standing in formation, helmets, M-14's, full packs, and exhausted after a full day of grenades and gas warfare training, and stale news. We actually got to throw a grenade. During gas warfare we went into a room full of tear gas and then took off the masks. Everyone just stood around, coughing and bawling like babies. Then we went into a chlorine gas room with our masks on. A 2nd time we entered the chlorine gas room with no masks on and held our breath until we were lined up in the room and then we put on the masks. It was a seven mile march each way. Chow in the field. Next week we spend going out to the rifle range. Tomorrow we have more bayonet and hand to hand.

Glad to hear about Clyde's scholarship and Jim's hockey and the trip to Springfield. It's past lights out so goodnite. More later.

10 Mar '66
　　It is taking a lot of time to write this so I'll just mail this when lights are out. Got a letter from Kit yesterday. Thanks a lot, Kit. Good to hear from you.
　　Roger wrote me again. He's decided to quit school after the quarter and work for a while until next Sept. when he'll decide if he'll return to college or wait awhile and join the Army.
　　Last couple of days have been pretty long and hard. Things are tightening up a bit.
　　Curley, my other Acting Sgt., isn't leaving after all. I don't recall if I told you before, but he had a tumor which might have been malignant which would mean certain crippling and perhaps death. But it turned out that it wasn't cancerous and also he saw his wife and got cheered up again, so he now plans to go on into Airborne and sort of revenge his brother's death. He's a pretty good guy.
　　Lately our platoon has been finishing 1st or 2nd in inspections. We also look the best when we're marching in company formation.
　　This girl from M.U. has been writing me, she's a girl I met on a blind date in December, who I took out a bunch of times before I left, and she's been keeping me in touch with Mizzou news. She also wants to go out with me when I come home on leave, so when I drive down to pick up my clothes, etc, at 3-Squares, I might stay a couple of days to see John, Ted and other buddies and also to take that girl out.
　　Never got the letter Clyde wrote, guess he got the wrong address. Still am trying to write him but man, they don't give us a lot of extra time. E.g., we get up at 5:00, have reveille at 5:15, eat and then fall out for field formation at 6:30. But we clean up between the end of chow to formation so no time there. We are in the field until about 5:00 p.m. or 6:00 p.m. and then eat after mail call. Then we must get to the barracks, clean up, do ½ hr P.T.

43

in the barracks, shine shoes, wash clothes, shower, clean
our rifles, fix up our other equipment, do details (or in my
case, supervise them) and go to bed at 9:00 p.m. So, we
have fairly full days.

There's a swell rumor that we'll get out a week
early and be home before Easter. It's probably just a result
of wishful thinking, but I sure hope it's true.

Today a Lt. Col. and Company Commander Captain Andraysiak inspected our barracks. I don't know how
they liked it, but all of a sudden the sgts. got real mean
and started really driving us so it must have been bad.

I'm glad Jim's team did so well in Springfield.
What positions are you playing this year? I bet it's still
forward, and probably center.

Everyone be sure to write me. I hope to see you
soon. I don't know when we'll be getting weekend passes,
but I'll bet in a few weeks we will.

Before I forget—I had been waiting 6 weeks to
see a typical, 3 war veteran, aged and strong, weathered
and hardened, half crazy and fanatically military. At the
gas chambers yesterday the master sgt. there was like this.
Boy, what a nut. But I felt sorry for him that he had become so ornery and hateful of people in general. Guess he
fought 1 war too many. (He's been in WWII, Korea and
Viet Nam). Once I saw John Wayne play a guy <u>exactly</u>
like this guy in a war movie. Remember the Captain in
the "Caine Mutiny?" Just like him. Always yelling and
screaming and glaring and hitting things (e.g., walls, his
hands, soldiers).

Well, I'll get this thing in the mail.

Scott

For Dad and Mom: I'm not sure if this pertains to me,
because I don't think I'm rebelling, but in case you do,
read this clipping from "Reader's Digest."

In Bondage
*I know a man who grew up in a stuffy atmos-
phere of Victorian piety, and who rebelled at an early age.
He is now 50 years old and still rebelling.*

*His old family home was cluttered; so his own
home is starkly simple. His parents were fanatically de-
vout; so he is fanatically irreligious. His relatives were
dogmatically conservative; so he is dogmatically radical.*

*This man thinks himself a "free soul." He thinks
he has burst the bonds of his enslavement to the past. But
he is wrong—for he is overreacting to the past, and is still
chained to it by his hostility.*

*To do exactly the opposite is a form of bondage.
The young man who rebels from Babbitry to Bohemian-
ism because it is exactly the opposite of what his father
tried to cram down his throat is allowing his decisions to
be made by somebody else.*

*To be free, in the fullest sense, does not mean to
reject what our fathers believed; it means to discriminate,
to select, to take on the difficult task of separating our
principles from our passions.*

*Each generation, in some measure, rebels against
the last. It is normal and natural and healthy. But it is
necessary to know that the aim of rebellion is peace within
the soul, and not perpetual revolt.*

*--Sydney J. Harris, <ins>Last Things</ins>
<ins>First</ins> (Houghton Mifflin, 1961)*

March 30, 1966

Clyde—

Got your letter. Sorry I haven't written sooner.

I like the Army so far. I'm an Acting Sergeant,
which doesn't mean a damn thing except that I get
bitched at when things get screwed up. Finished 5 weeks
so far. Qualified as a sharpshooter on the range. Getting

45

bigger and stronger. Am still a cherry—so not -too deep in sin.

This girl I met on a blind date in December has been writing me regularly. She likes me pretty much –but I'm not going to get involved. Pam, the girl I had been real serious about when she shot me down four months ago, wrote and said she couldn't eat or shit or anything for 2 days after she found out I had joined. I wrote back and told her that if she had written out of courtesy, I wish she hadn't. She waited a couple of days, to test her reaction, and wrote back and said she wanted to see me and some other stuff. I think she likes me a lot. We had been counting on marriage before, and I never stopped liking her, so no telling what will happen. Nothing till after I get out of the Army, tho. I figure 3 years would test something. Enough of this shit.

Dad said, and your letter implied, that you may or may not be in college Sept. I hope the Marines defer you until you get thru law school.

Wed., 30

This letter is kind of slow, so I'll write as much as I can until formation and mail it tonight. 15 days and we'll be thru.

I went home Sat. nite on a 24 hr pass. It wasn't for very long but it was good to see everyone and catch up on all the news. Last Sunday, Jan and Becky came down. Becky's engaged to this guy here and we bombed around in a convertible with the stereo in it and played Sandy Nelson. Jan has been seeing this doctor every week. A couple weeks ago she had another escapade but she seems lots better. She's a swell girl and I hope she gets straightened out soon.

Thurs. –31

Just got paid $80. 14 days till graduation.

Hope you're having a good time—lots of luck with that girl.

Scott

Tues 10 May 66

Clyde—

Got home last weekend. The illness I had picked up last week made me feel really bad Sunday, so mom took me to the hospital to have it diagnosed. It turned out to be acute tonsillitis. The doctor gave me a shot of penicillin in the ass and told me to go on sick call when I get back to my base. I did and he put me on light indoor duty, gave me some medicine and told me to come again the next day. It is very hard to speak, eat or sleep with tonsillitis, so I've been getting rundown quick. When I went back the next day (today) he asked if I felt any better. Not really able to tell, optimistically I said, "yes, a little". He then congratulated me on my miraculous recovery and told me to get the hell back to my unit.

So, I'm sicker than hell and I'm back on regular duty. In our first week we climbed 30'-35' poles. Last Fri., we were tested on it. The high scorers will be sent to Ft. Gordon, Ga., for a different MOS (Military Occupation Status). My present MOS deals with setting up temporary communications; Ft. Gordon will teach us permanent communications set-up. With the experience I'll get there, it will be easy to get a high paying job as a lineman for a telephone company.

Wed 11 66 May

Hallelujah! We finally got paid today! It had been a whole month and a ½.

This girl, Barb? Who I met (euphemism—picked up) last December and took out last month asked me to the Rosati Kane High Prom. Tragically**I had to decline because we generally don't get passes here until Sat. and the Prom is Fri., 13th. Alas! I only hope I didn't break the dear girl's heart. Life is so full of heartbreak and frustration.

Another girl, also Barb something or other, whom I met (picked up) on Thanksgiving and again in

December, ran into me and an Army buddy last weekend
at the Washington U Carnival. Her forced exchange of
addresses, my forced promise to write, and her damp eyes
tell me that she has romantic designs on me (shudder).
Well, right now I am so damned disgusted at the opposite
sex (damn that BITCH Eve!) that the usually attachable
Scott cannot get interested in either Barb.

Obviously the thing that soured me on the subject is a frustrating experience with Pam. After the first
few dates I became more than mildly interested in Pam.
After a reasonable length of time we mutually and rather
hilariously decided that we liked each other enough to
eventually get married. Later she shot my ass down because of what I learned, several months later, resulted
from a bad mood. I hadn't seen or heard from her for a
couple months when she began writing me. On a weekend pass we discovered that with a few minor adjustments,
nothing had changed and that it had actually grown. (Let
me insert here that never before had I been so snowed over
a girl that I would consider marriage.) It was no typical
snow job because our relationship had developed into a
very serious, joyful, occasionally argumentative, realistic,
childish (e.g. wrestling in the graveyard after a nominal
consumption of Apricot Brandy), carefree, mutually en-
riching and intercourseless love. (The latter was decided to
be saved for later.) Needless to say, when several weeks
after I saw her on the weekend pass, I found out that she
had been regularly sleeping with a Bagpipe player from
Gaslight Square. I was so shocked, pissed off and angry at
everything manmade (buildings, cars, streets, unhappi-
ness, disappointment, airplanes, love, sons of men, sky
scrapers, bridges, Hugh Hefner's full of shit philosophy,
and burnt eggs) that I decided that when I could I would
live on a small farm far far from man's corrupt cities.

While wallowing in my pissedoffidness, I found
within myself two conflicting thots. (1) being that man
was an S.O.B. and (2) that unless man was basically good,

48

things look awful dismal for us. Objectively looking at his constructive and genuinely happy and numerous achievements and the concept of a good God, I have tentatively accepted that beneath the often shitty, sometimes wonderful crust of Life pie, there lies a happy, full-filling. (Note the talented play on words in the last part of the previous sentence.)

By the way, I felt similar throbs of anguish in your letter you sent to our house. Don't feel like the Lone Ranger. Same agony, just different situations.

So, stay tuned to this same neurotic station, and find out whether or not man is good or evil. Being tentatively in a frame of mind filled with confidence in the basic nature of man, the producer of the 2-bit soap opera confronts the viewer with a question to answer the above question.

Does shit stink?

Your ever confused brother,

Scott

p.s. Hearty congrats on your achievements at Stanford

13 May 66

Hello!

Greetings & Salutations!

Despite the efforts of these veterinarians, I appear to be healing.

Rejoice! I have been rewarded by the government of the USA for one month's valiant service. Enclosed find one feeble attempt, crude as it is, to repay youse.

Bon voyage! For the 28th of May will see yours truly venture forth to Georgia. Ft. Gordon to be exact.

Expect me home for Jan's birthday. Tomorrow I will probably go to Iowa and stay with either Jim Baxter or Bob Miller, another guy from B42.

Please send me Jan's address.

Briefly yours--

Scott

DOGPATCH HILLBILLY FARM
Lake Ozark, Missouri
Located near Bagnell Dam on U. S. Hwy. 54
Children from 6 to 60 will enjoy the exhibits at
Dogpatch.

Post Card

WASHINGTON 5¢
UNITED STATES

OSAGE BEACH, MO.
MAY 16
AM
1966
65065

Hello everybody —
Decided to relax
the weekend so Jim + I
+ Miller came up here +
spent Sat + Sun here. We got
a good hotel right near the
water. Lots of soldiers
here. I'll be home next
weekend. Like I said in the
letter. He 28th we go to
Ft. Gordon.
                Scott

Christofferson's
3 Thorndell
St. Louis 17, Mo

dp DEXTER PRESS, INC.
WEST NYACK, NEW YORK

71853-B

50

Chapter IV.
Fort Gordon, Georgia

Wed 1 June 66

Hello—

Got here Sun. 1:30 a.m. Did nothing over the weekend except see movies and go swimming. The "10th Victim" is real good. Sean Connery in "A Fine Madness" is great. That is a terrific flick.

First day of classes today. 5 hrs. classes and 3 hrs. pole climbing. 30 ft. poles again. This will be a 6 week course, a week longer than I expected. While I was being processed-in, I was assured of Airborne School—if I passed the PT test. But because of my score in basic, I doubt if I'll have to take the test at all.

Dad: I'd like to have your opinion on an Insurance policy offered to us. It's the Rio Grande National Life Insurance Company (Dallas). The Death Benefit is $10,000 and the annual premium is $113.50. If not cancelled, after 3 years the policy is paid for (and will cover you for the next 20 years even when cancelled after 3 years). A cash value starts and increases to $2,090.00 after 20 years. 20 years of premiums comes to $2,270.00. It has no restrictions as to "occupation, aviation, military or naval service, travel or residence in time of peace or war."

How does this compare with other Life Insurance policies?

Is the idea of a Life Insurance policy favorable at all for me?

Wouldn't an injury, theft or damage policy be a lot more

useful?

If either mom or dad wants to comment on this, please do. Knowing how often dad writes (about as often as the moon turns blue) have mom put his comments in one of her letters. I am totally ignorant on such things and would appreciate your ideas on the subject.

The weather here is hot and sunny. The ground is sandy in many places and we're a hundred miles from Savannah. Augusta is 15 miles from here. It's a pretty good post and the food is good. We're off duty and have time to ourselves at 5:30. We're up at 4:30. Lots of pine trees. Flat compared to Missouri. Jim Baxter and I are in the same tent (Each holds 18 people) and when we get paid we plan to go to Savannah.

Well, I better sign off.

Scott

20 June 66

Hi Clyde—

How's it going? I got a card from Mom (Seattle) and she said you got home Monday. What kind of a job did you get? Congrats on your graduation. By the way what kind of diploma (degree) did you get? How's things going with that girl of yours? If there's any one thing I could pick that I missed most about army life it is the lack of involvement with females. The only relationship possible here is always short and usually meaningless.

Weekends here have been pretty damn dull— mostly on account of we weren't paid until a few days ago. School's going good. Pole line construction, telephone installation, switchboards, etc., etc.

Enclosed are a few snaps I took with a $18.50 polaroid I bought. Have them saved around the house— I'll need them for my memoirs.

Let me know what you're doing. I should get my orders next week.

Scott

22 June 66

Hi Everybody—

It's 6:00 a.m. now and I have a half hour until duty formation. We got up at 4:30 as usual and ate. Since nothing's been happening I don't have too much to say, but since I had the time I thought I'd write to solicit letters.

We got paid on Friday so my money shortage is ended, if only temporarily. I put some in the bank and also bought a 15 second Swinger Polaroid Camera. It works pretty good, and at the price ($18.50) and convenience, it's unbeatable. I sent some pictures with my letter to Clyde, telling him to have them saved for posterity. Speaking of pictures, if you have some snapshots of anybody there be sure to send them to me. Everyone else is always showing off their families' pictures and I haven't one in my wallet.

We should get our orders next week, so when I find out what they are, I'll write then and let you know.

Scott

7 July 66

Hello everyone—

Got my orders yesterday—Ft. Benning for Airborne. Today I process, tomorrow I graduate, and Sat. I report to Ft. Benning. So I guess Monday I'll start jump school. That means I won't get a leave until I go overseas, so I should get home in early August, after Airborne. If everything goes o.k., I'll graduate from Jump School July 29. It's going to be a real challenge, physically and mentally, but I know I'm up to it. We haven't done any P.T. at all here, but I've been working out on my own and have gotten so I can do 50 pushups with no strain at all. And I

53

took that Airborne PT test 3 times—they kept losing my records. So I'm in pretty good shape. I'm in the right frame of mind too.

These last two weeks have been real easy. Mostly just setting up commo[1] systems on Brigade level.

Yesterday I got a package of cookies and brownies from the Lautman's.

Bill Owens (an MP here who was in my platoon in basic) and myself and Jim Baxter went to Savannah Beach for the weekend of the 4th. That's quite a place and swimming in the ocean was a great thrill. No kidding, the ocean is the most beautiful thing.

The other day during a break out at the Ponderosa (our name for the place we set up commo systems) I was listening to a career sgt. talking with a pvt. about Army food. The pvt., typically, was complaining about Army life in general and Army food in particular. The sgt. was defending Army life in general and Army food in particular. The sgt. replied to the pvt.'s charges that the food was lousy with saying that rarely was food poisoning found in Army camps, while food poisoning was frequent on the outside. The pvt. said: "It isn't surprising that there isn't any food poisoning in the Army. Hell, Army food is so sorry that it won't hold poison."

Maybe it'll be interesting to see what orders look like, so I enclosed a copy of mine.

Scott

---

[1] *Army slang for communications*

209. TC 221. Fol rsg dir. WP TDN 2172010 01-1151-1153 P1411 899-999
CHRISTOFFERSON SCOTT A RA17729663 PVT E2 36C20
  Rel fr: Tng Co M USATCS (3A-3165-07) this sta
  Asg to: 4th Stu Bn Stu Bde (3151) Ft Benning Ga for ABN Tng
  WP: o/a 8 Jul 66
  Rept date: 9 Jul 66
  Scty clnc: FINAL SECRET
  PCS(MDC): IL
  Auth: DA LTR OPO (No 7-8)
  ADC: 3 yrs
  BASD: Jan 66
  BPED: Jan 66
  ETS: Jan 69
  DEPN: 0
  PPSC: A
  EDCSA: 9 Jul 66
  MODE OF TVL: TC will furn nec trans and AMT.
  SP INSTR: UP Sec V Ch 2 AR 600-200 & upon compl of crs on 8 Jul 66 indiv
       awd & dsg PMOS 36C20. Indiv will rept to Bldg 28501 for final
       clnc prior to departure fr this comd. When MATS or coml air
       trans util 19 lbs excess bag auth.

          FOR THE COMMANDANT:

OFFICIAL: MAURICE J. CASTILLE
                                    LTC, Signal Corps
                                    Secretary

G. E. GODBEE
CW4, USA
Asst Adjutant

DISTRIBUTION:
  30-Pay Br Pers Div
  30-Rec Unit Stu Br Pers Div
  30-Proc Br Pers Div
  15-Tng Co M Z
   5-4th Stu Bn Stu Bde Ft Benning Ga
   5-CO OS Repl Sta Ft Dix NJ
   5-SC STRAT COM PHUIM APO SF 96243
   3-Admin Co

Chapter V.
Airborne

16 July 66

Hello Everyone—

AN OVERALL IMPRESSION

This morning while I was policing up cigarette butts in the company area and reflecting over all the unnecessary harassment of the past week, I became angered over the fact that as of yet I haven't done anything for national defense, freedom or anything else in the 6 months that I've been in the Army. But now that I think more on the subject, I feel much better. My training will be over in two weeks. After that I'll become a useful soldier, capable of doing an important job for one of the U.S.'s key units— the Airborne. Altho I still have two hard weeks ahead of me, the end is in sight, at long last, for the time that I'll be only a Trainee. Soon I'll be a useful soldier.

AN IMPRESSION OF AIRBORNE TRAINING

Although not nearly as strenuous as I had expected, Airborne is indeed a rough course. Last week was the hardest 5 days of continuous work I've ever done. My muscles are sore, especially the leg muscles, and I am quite tired. I plan to spend most of the weekend sleeping and reading and writing.

Next week is Tower Week. We'll go up 250' towers and be dropped off in an already opened parachute. It will be our first sample of actual falling with a parachute. The week after that will be Jump Week, in which we will make 5 jumps from 1250 feet. The first couple will be individual jumps, the last few will be "mass exits."

This was Ground Week. Every day we ran a few miles, did some P.T., and then trained for the rest of the day. Thurs. & Fri. we got up at 3:00. The other days we got up at 4:30. The training consisted of:
1: practice exits from mock doors 2' off the ground.
2. exits from a 34' tower. Our harnesses were attached to a trolly on a cable. It was fun after the first jump.
3. Parachute Landing Falls. There are basically 4 ways you will hit the ground in a parachute jump. Moving to the front, rear, left or right. Since you're traveling 17' per second, it's important to know how to hit the ground. Most serious injuries here result from hitting the ground incorrectly.

The biggest problem here is heat. Every hour we must take salt pills & fully clothed showers to keep us from getting heat exhaustion. Despite these precautions, daily men are evacuated by helicopter after collapsing. The heat is toughest for the older men and the people not used to it.

There's all kinds of men in this place. Rank all the way from Pvt. to Major. We train side by side as equals. One Major, three or four Captains, a couple of 1st lieutenants, 20 or so 2nd Lts., including Marine and Naval personnel. There are also Sgts., staff sgts. and spec 4's. Because the Army gives Airborne training to all the services, we have Air Force cadets here, Marines and Navy people. 500 people in the class.

There are a bunch of Marine Lts. here who need Airborne status for advanced Reconnaissance. Tell Clyde I think that's what he should do. Among other things, the $55 extra Parachute Pay would make it worthwhile.

I should be getting my PFC stripes in a few weeks. With the pay increase plus Jump pay, I'll be making twice as much money as when I first came in. I looked in my records and found out that I did make E-2 after basic, but the Finance dep't. messed up and only paid me E-1 pay for a month or so. I'll have some money from that coming in soon.

I didn't come here with anyone I knew. (Jim Baxter didn't have his orders when I left, by the way) but I met 2 guys here I went to LOC with. I also ran into a fellow I met in Basic—he was on crutches.

We had a Special Forces talk the other day. I believe that if I didn't have to wait until I was 20 to be eligible, I would've signed up for it. As it is, I won't ever be a Green Beret because I'd have to reenlist for 3 years to meet the qualifications—and I definitely don't plan to do that. Definitely.

In the class that just graduated, the linesmen went to the 82nd (not in Viet Nam). Most everyone else got assigned to the 101st (Viet Nam). 173rd (S.V.N.) 1st Cav. (Airmobile, also in S.V.N.). Altho 90% went to Viet Nam, I have no idea where my orders will send me. I do hope I go to Viet Nam, tho, because among other reasons, I'll get a leave, whereas most people going other places don't get one.

A big organization like the Army is likely to foul up. It does. But it also tells the public lies. It said that all Army personnel will get leaves after AIT whether or not they go overseas or stateside. I can name 10 guys right now in Germany that had no leaves after Lineman school. The Army also claims that no 17-year-olds are in Viet Nam. I know 3 17-year-olds who got orders to go there after lineman school. It also says that personnel returning from Viet Nam will get their preference in stateside post assignments. The "Army Times" recently published figures estimating that only 30% of these people actually get their preferences. These three examples of how the Army breaks promises just goes to show that the needs of the Army (based and regulated according to the needs of the Army in Viet Nam) are above its promises. Which is not necessarily a bad thing—just an unavoidable thing with things as they are.

Enough about the Army.

58

ASSORTED TRIVIA

In this month's Readers Digest is an article about the Alaska Highway. It, judging from my own experience, is a very accurate article about that road. It is also an informative article that gives the road's history, as well as its present condition.

I quit the Columbia Record Club. In the service I can purchase records, stereo or mono, for only $2.39, as opposed to $4.79 for records from the Record Club.

I have greatly appreciated the letters I've gotten from home. Jim's one letter, Carrie's several, Kit's letter, Carl's letter, and Frank's were all priceless. One in particular I enjoyed is Carl's laboriously type-written letter, which I assure you will be printed in my memoirs exactly as it was written.

Someone stole one of my fatigue pants off the clothesline.

That TR-4 of Clyde's must be something.

It's hard to believe that Jim will be in junior high in a couple of months.

Material for my biography is gathering quickly.

Don't expect me home until I ring the doorbell.

Scott

Keep writing.

21 July 66

Hello Everybody—

I am now at the close of my second week of Airborne training. Right now I'm on fireguard—which means I stay up for an hour watching for nonexistent fires.

Altho harder than the first week, the second week has gone faster. Monday and Tuesday we did Parachute Landing Falls from the sling harness trainer; mass exits from 34' towers; the 8 preparatory commands prior to jumping while in a mock airplane; operation of the risers in a suspended harness; and other things. Wednesday we had our first real sense of parachuting with a free fall of 250'—which seems a considerable height when you're hanging at the top of the tower praying nothing will break.

Altho the fall was relatively short, 1/5th of our jumps next week, it was thrilling. It's a great feeling to look up and see the main chute billowing overhead. The sensation of a retarded falling is fantastic. I can't wait until next week when we jump from 1250'.

Tomorrow, Friday, should be easier than the rest of the week. I shall again relax during the weekend. Monday and Tuesday we should jump 3 times, and Wednesday, the other 2 times. The last jump will be with full equipment—field pack and weapon included. Thursday will be graduation day (should I get by without a busted head or anything). By then we should have our orders. Speculation on my orders is useless but unavoidable. I have found that there is a chance I won't be assigned to an Airborne unit, which would mean I'd be Airborne qualified but working with a regular unit. Most likely, tho, judging from where other linemen have gone, I'll be assigned to the 82nd. This is, however, pure speculation on my part.

When I get paid at the end of the month, I'll get $32.50 of my jump pay. For a full month I'll get $55.

(letter ended here and never was mailed; it was found among his effects later)

Fri 29 July 66

Hi!

Thot you might be interested in the class book. Also, here are a couple of diplomas, and a picture of yours truly exactly as I appear when ready to jump.

For some reason we won't be shipping to Brooklyn until tomorrow, which suits me fine, as it'll give me more time to pack and write letters. The people in charge here have conflicting words as to what will happen to us when we get there (Germany). One NCO says we'll just train for several months to make us combat ready, then ship to Nam. This, however, pertains mostly to infantry men. He says Signal Corps like me will have a good chance of staying. The other NCO in charge says most everybody will become permanent party there. Either way it looks like I have a good chance of : 1. Being in an Airborne unit, either in Germany or Nam, which is an important thing to me. I don't want to go to a leg unit. (A "leg," incidentally, is the Airborne's uncomplimentary way of referring to a non-airborne. And if you aren't Airborne, you just aren't with it.); 2. being stationed in Germany. This suits me fine because I'll have ample chance to take in the sights. With a good sized leave over there, I could see a lot of Europe.

If I find I will be there in Germany (the tour of duty there is 18 months to 2 years) I will buy a mode of transportation so I can travel around. It would be either a motorcycle or an economical car, like a VW. This would have the added advantage of military transportation (for the vehicle) when I return to the U.S. – tax free.

If I do go to Viet Nam from Germany, as there is some reason to believe, I could get back to St. Louis much sooner because the tour of duty there is only 12 months.

Either way, Germany or Viet Nam, things will be exciting and new for me. So I'll just cast my fate to the wind and take whatever comes.

Scott

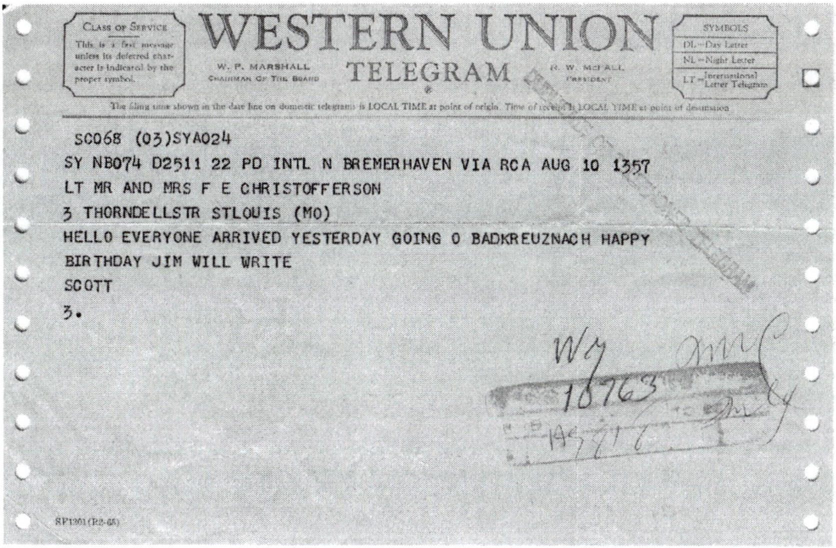

CLASS OF SERVICE
This is a fast message unless its deferred character is indicated by the proper symbol.

WESTERN UNION
TELEGRAM

W. P. MARSHALL
CHAIRMAN OF THE BOARD

R. W. MCFALL
PRESIDENT

SYMBOLS
DL=Day Letter
NL=Night Letter
LT=International Letter Telegram

The filing time shown in the date line on domestic telegrams is LOCAL TIME at point of origin. Time of receipt is LOCAL TIME at point of destination

SC068 (03)SYA024
SY NB074 D2511 22 PD INTL N BREMERHAVEN VIA RCA AUG 10 1357
LT MR AND MRS F E CHRISTOFFERSON
3 THORNDELLSTR STLOUIS (MO)
HELLO EVERYONE ARRIVED YESTERDAY GOING O BADKREUZNACH HAPPY
BIRTHDAY JIM WILL WRITE
SCOTT
3.

Chapter VI.
Germany

Thurs. 18 Aug 66

Hello everyone—

 Here's what's happened since the 28th of July:
 First of all, we didn't leave for New York until
Sunday night of the 31st. We left at midnight and got to
JFK airport at about 8:00 a.m. A bus took us to the pier
in Brooklyn & after wasting time for a while we boarded
the USNS General Rose. It was a troop ship—1800 men
in all. Crowded as heck. Bunks 4 high and jampacked
together. We left at 4:00 that afternoon, and on the way
out we saw the Statue of Liberty and the somehow unreal
spectacle of Manhattan Island. We were told we would
get to Bremerhaven on the following Tuesday. With the
exception of one rough nite, the trip was calm and
smooth. I spent most of my time either sleeping in hidden
corners of the ship (to avoid getting nabbed for details),
reading books from the ship library, or on the deck watching what was to be seen. I didn't get nabbed for any details. I read some short stories by A.B. Guthrie; and a
collection of 28 of F. Scott Fitzgerald's short stories. Fitzgerald's stories were in chronological order, which was
very revealing about his own life, and accompanied by
editor's notes on the Author. I don't remember the title,
but if you ever get a chance, read it. A treasury of the
Theatre contained, among others, "Golden Boy, " "The
Hairy Ape," "The Glass Menagerie," and the tremendous,
"Death of a Salesman," which was by far the most dramatic and meaningful play I've read. It has fantastic impact and power and I very much would like to see it on

the stage.

From the deck there wasn't much to be seen, except for occasional merchant ships. Towards the end of the voyage, however, the shipping increased, and at times we saw coastlines of both sides of the English Channel. Not both at the same time, of course, because the Channel is too wide in most places, but we saw the southernmost tip of the British Isles at one point, and later on we could see some part of France. It was a fine trip and someday I'd like to do more traveling by sea.

We arrived in Bremerhaven at 7:00 on Tuesday Aug. 9. Apparently we caused some excitement among the Germans because many of them lined the pier. We tried communicating with them, but had little success. On Wednesday we left the ship for the first time in 9 days and boarded a train. Only 400 or so were on the train to Bad Kreuznach. The rest split up and went to places like Berlin and even as far away as Italy. We got to Bad Kreuznach the next morning.

Bad Kreuznach is a small town that exactly fits my idea of what a tiny German village should look like. The streets are sort of cobblestone, which provides a stunning effect when contrasted with the multi-colored, slope-roofed little houses which line the streets. Flowers and trees are everywhere, which adds to the colorful effect. The people dress differently from Americans—wearing baggier, more conservative clothes, and show ruddy complexions and fair sized bodies. There is, or appears to be, always someone working in the many gardens behind and alongside the houses. There is a high ridge on both sides of the town. It is farmland and pasture, and neatly sectioned off into long rectagonal lots. It is a picturesque town right out of a picture book, and marred only by one thing: The American G.I.'s. On the eastern side of town is an area fenced off which contains the Rose Barracks (No relation to the ship, I don't think). Here, the 8th Inf. Div. of M.P.s; the Adjutant General's Typing School; the 8th

Div. Replacement Company; and the 8th Div. Signal Battalion reside. It is a crime, an actual crime, that these interlopers are allowed to clutter up the otherwise beautiful countryside. The rude boom of cannons for reveille and retreat, the ruckus of the many trucks of the Sig. B., constantly going in and out of town; and the unforgivable hell-raising of the bored G.I.s constitute, to me, an unpardonable offense to the tranquility of these German people, and a sin against the beauty of the land. I may be an American soldier here working in the Signal Battalion, 8th Inf. Division, but I condemn the presence of all U.S. G.I.'s here anyway. I don't think a foreigner should be permitted to litter up this beautiful countryside. Uncle Sam is perhaps the worst litterbug the world has ever seen. Just think! While United States beauty-minded anti-litter committees are having spaz attacks about paper cups alongside of highways in America, just think of all the thousands and thousands of ugly O.D. colored vehicles and men swarming across German soil, contaminating the land they walk on. It is amazing the Germans can contain themselves to the small show of resentment they, on occasion, display. If it was me I'd be up in arms...

Either they ought to put the U.S. posts in the German wastelands (if such wastelands exist in this country) or throw them out of the country. I can see why De-Gaulle asked us to leave France. It wasn't a matter of NATO and all that; really, it was a move to beautify France. After all, wasn't Paris a nice place before we got there?

After totally denouncing United States presence in Germany (and by implication, all foreign countries) I'll turn to other matters.

I like it here, although I sincerely regret that I'm here as a U.S. litter bug. However, on leaves I won't be a litterbug because I will buy a bicycle (there are thousands of bikes here) and unobtrusively meander along out-of-the-way roads, just admiring the natural beauty of Germany. I'll let my hair grow long (as long as the Army will allow, however), dress as Germans do and even learn a little Deutsch. That way I won't uglify the place and I'll see the country and I won't be a gum chewing, shutterbug, leering, drunken G.I.

Barring an unforeseen event, like if for Christmas Uncle Sam gives me a discharge, which I doubt, I'll be here until 20 days before my discharge date. That makes it about two years and 5 months before I'll be home again. By that time, Jim will be in the 9th grade, Carrie in the 7th, Kit finishing grade school, and Carl and Frank a whole 2 1/2 years older. I guess by the next time I see you all, things will have changed. I'll be 21 and going back to college, Clyde will be in his last year of law school, just about to go into the Marines. I don't know what Jan will be doing then, but I'm sure it will be interesting. Mom and Dad will still be hard at work being good parents, and the St. Louis Cards will probably still be a mediocre 5th. The Mississippi will still be muddy, the weather will still be neurotic, and Uncle Sam will still be a litterbug.

About my job: I am one of the relatively few Airborne personnel with the 8th Signal Battalion, 8th Inf. Div. I work an 8 hr. day as in a regular job. After 4:30 p.m. I can do anything I want. There's a library here, so I think I'll be spending most of my free time reading and writing. If I get so inspired I'll even buy a watercolor set and do some painting. The University of Maryland offers a few courses and maybe I'll take one or two. A Parachuting Club is on post and I might join that. A movie house is on post—tomorrow they will show "The Knack." Once a month the battalion goes to the field for 3 to 10 days. We leave this Friday for my first time.

All in all, this ought to be an interesting tour of duty.

Be sure to write and keep me up on things.

Scott

My address

> *Pvt. Scott A. Christofferson RA 17729663*
> *Aco 8th Sig. Bn. 8th Inf. Div*
> *APO New York 09111*

21 Sept. 66

Hello—

Just came in off duty from Kubourg (sp?) Hill. We had a commo set up there and I was on shift working the patch panel. It's 12:00 a.m. and I have the rest of the day off.

Got a letter from Jan, starts off July8, ends up Aug. 28 and is real cool—the time element was dramatic.

Particularly good flick—"A Slender Thread"

10 day field problem coming up in October. Time really flies. Just a year ago I was in the second week at Mizzou.

Say hello to everybody and send Jan's address. Also send Clyde's.

Scott

24 Sept 66

Hi Ted—

Christ! They must be drafting a lot of college guys in the states. I didn't know that they were down to that already. If they let you alone till the school year is finished it might be wise to go OCS and be an officer for your tour of duty. Being an officer is good. However, I'm happy as a lowly PFC. Few responsibilities, no morals whatsoever, and absolutely no sense at all. Being an EM has its advantages too.

I doubt if they'll pull the 8th Inf. Div. out of Europe to go to Viet Nam. This will suit me fine. My views on the war have changed considerably.

I don't think that any of the other services are any better, but the Army sucks. The only really worthwhile thing I've done yet is go to Airborne School. Parachuting is a big thrill. They have a skydivers club on Post and I'm going to join. Right now I'm not getting jump pay ($55 a month) because there isn't a slot open for me yet. Altho, since I've come here, my name has moved up on the list to #2, so it shouldn't be more than a few months until I start jumping for pay.

Made PFC this month. A Pvt. E-1 makes about $93, Pvt. E-2 makes about $100, and PFC makes around $120 a month.

It sounds like you had a great summer—going to Canada and all. Did your whole family go? What's JJ doing? Clyde's in law school now. He got a 3-yr. deferment from the Marines. I don't know if I told you before, but he's going to Stanford's Law school on scholarship. He bought a TR-4 this summer. Jan's living in an apartment now and is going to Junior College. She has a Honda 50. I can't even believe that Jim is in 7th grade. He's almost as old as we were when we knew Sue, Ann, Debby, etc. etc. Speaking of Sue, I really fucked up good with her and I feel like an ass. When I was on leave last April I guess I told Roger too much about Sue—just bullshitting around, talking about things and people we knew—well, it happened that Roger was working with Sue's hubby, and he said something he shouldn't have. I can't figure why the hell he'd of done it unless he's just stupid, but Roger said something to Sue's husband about what she had done once, and that nite I got a call from him. He was pissed off like he should have been and I felt lower than whale shit. I've learned my lesson to keep my goddamn mouth quiet, tho, but I think I lost a good friend, Roger, and I know I've acquired two enemies, Sue and her husband. Like I said, I feel like quite an ass about the whole thing. Shit.

69

As much as I dislike the Army I'll admit that I've got it pretty good here. We're on a tiny post, only the 8th Sig Bn (600 men), an MP detachment and the division headquarters; outside of Bad Krueznach, a town of 30,000. The town is beautiful—a river runs thru it and there is farmland and hills all around it. On post is a bowling alley, movie house, EM club (30 cents for a good Tom Collins, 15 cents for German beer), a service club (which contains pool tables and craft shop, musical instruments , a library and other crap) and a terrific athletic department. A fully equipped gym, track and baseball and football fields make for lots to do.

As far as what we do on duty, the average day is spent in the motor pool working (actually, *looking* like we are working) on our trucks and equipment for 8 hours. I am a driver of a deuce and a half and am responsible for that truck. I should make Spec. 4 in three or four months. The pay for s Spec 4 is around $160. Once a month we go to the field for anywhere from 3 to 10 days. It isn't bad out there and it provides a break to the monotony of the place.

When I get paid at the end of the month I'll buy a camera and send some pictures. It's a beautiful country (and the girls—wow!). However, the girls are afraid of G.I.s and there don't seem to be any cat houses in town, so on pay day me and some guys plan to go to Frankfurt and indulge in plenty of sin.

Passes are simple as hell to get and the only reason you won't get them is if you are in trouble. Leaves are easy to get, too, if you have any time coming to you. 30 days for each year. I'll have a total of 77 days coming to me in the next 28 months and I plan to see a lot of Europe.

A brand new VW costs 5,600 marks ($1,400 dollars) and when I make Spec. 4 I'll plan to buy one. It'll cost only $160 to ship it back to the U.S. so I'll be coming out ahead.

I don't think I'll go back to the States until Jan.
'69 when the Army will send me back for (oh joy!) Separation! Receiving my Honorable Discharge will make me
the happiest person alive. I really look forward to getting
back to college and FREEDOM.

Write me when you get a chance and let me
know what's going on.

Scott

P.S. I can't visualize you in uniform HA! HA! (Try
smoking an ink saturated cigarette before the physical or
taking some pills or alcohol to mess them up. The ink
would make your lungs look like hell and the booze would
give you too high blood pressure.) Actually I don't recommend this.

1 Oct 66

Hi ya Clyde!

How's it going? Your car running ok? What's
the story on that girl?

I made PFC last month. I should make Spec. 4
by January and I should get put on jump status real soon.
This would mean $55 more per month. As PFC I make
(before tax allotments, etc.) $129 or so. As Spec. 4 it
would be $160. I'm considering buying a car over here.
A brand new VW costs $1400. To ship it home would be
around $160 more. I'll have 77 days leave coming before
I rotate back to the States, and if I had a car I could really
see the country.

I'm glad Jan's back in school. I just hope she
sticks with it. I'm sure she'll make it all right.

Say—while reading a month-old copy of the San
Gabriel Valley Daily News I saw an ad for a speed reading
course. It had examples of students' before and after reading speed. Guess who was one of the students? I sent the

clipping home for Mom and Dad's benefit.

Not much happening except that this month we have a 10-day field problem. Only 846 days left!

Scott

--don't know your address, so I'll send this to St. Louis. Hope it gets to you on time.

HAPPY BIRTHDAY

3 Oct 66

Hello everyone—

Well. Nothing much has been happening. Been reading books, writing essays (mostly on Army life) short stories, and been going to shows. And once in a while a game of chess. I'm proud that I play a good enough game against everybody- and beat most everyone. One guy from Brooklyn, however, is too good for me.

I've been playing with the company flag football team, and we are 1-1.

Saturday (after a big inspection) I went to Frankfurt. Real cool town. The train there (60 miles) was great. The town is pretty big and industrious and busy, but I much prefer small villages like B.K. Much less corrupted by the G.I. dollar and doesn't cater to G.I.'s fancy quite so much.

We've got a 10 day field problem coming up this month.

By November I should be on jump status. By Jan. or Feb. I should be a Spec. 4. Both these things would mean considerably more money than I'm making now, which I'll bank. There's a 10% interest on savings for servicemen overseas. I haven't been using this yet and have been depositing to my bank in Columbia, mainly because if I wasn't to draw some $ out and buy something or go somewhere (I'm contemplating a 1967 trip home) I'd be unable to take it out of the gov't savings bank—whereas I can draw upon my Columbia account at any time. I figured the loss in interest difference at around $200, but I consider the convenience more valuable. The 10% plan is in an effort to slow down the gold flow by GIs overseas, and your account can't be used until you return to the States, or have an emergency.

In case I haven't told you before, I eventually did buy that GI insurance policy I mentioned (which will eventually cover my wife and kids, if and when I get some) guaranteed in peace or war. It cannot rise above the $9.40 monthly premiums, which is the main reason I bought it. The company is one of several who grouped together to insure G.I.s under a plan similar to the one in W.W.II. It's the Commercial Bankers Life Insurance Company, 863 Mittee Road, Burlingame, California. If you've heard anything about the company that makes it sound unstable, please let me know.

I got a letter from Jan, and await the one from Clyde that Mom mentioned. Ted Myrick wrote me and said he's been reclassified 1-A and should be drafted by next summer. John's written regularly and seems to be doing fine. Carrie's "Mag" was great: She's got a genuine talent for writing. Frank's writing has drastically improved and I got a kick out of his letter. The "Beatle Bailey" clippings Kit sent now reside inside the doors of my wall locker, among God-knows what else.

Say, what has become of the Lautmans being sent to Munich? Be sure and let me know.

Things here have settled down to a pretty dull routine, and I'm looking forward to the field problem to break it up.

Will write, and you keep writing too.

Scott

P.S. Only 843 days left!

10 Oct '66

Dear Dad,

I had a hearty and happy laugh. You will, too, when you realize this letter is my first to you alone.

Thanks for forwarding your mom's letter; I have gotten two others from her and I appreciate them all.

You did not misinterpret my "litterbug" message, and if you were here I am certain you would share it.

Before I got your letter I wrote Jan a letter in care of home. Of course, I didn't know she was in St. Mary's, but it would be a good letter for her anyway and I hope you forwarded it. The hard object in the envelope was my "bloodwings," a thing traditionally sent to a loved one.

Knowing your uncanny ability to sense what is going on in my mind, I can't help but think your letter was prompted by your concern over what I am doing and what I am going to do. Incidentally, in case I never told you before, your perceptive insight in this manner is amazing—and not unappreciated.

Being in the Army, as you know, exposes me to things I hadn't been exposed to before.

I know what alcohol is. It only took me a couple of times of waking up the next morning feeling like hell to make me realize the virtue of Ben Franklin's idea on the subject, the gist of which was: don't drink to elevation.

For the simple reasons that I have seen what cigarettes do to people's wind and health, and besides, I can't stand the awful taste it leaves in my mouth, I do not smoke.

As far as women are concerned, all I can say is I am not a Boy Scout.

That covers the present.

I have a strong feeling that you already have suspected and perhaps openly voiced what I'll tell you next.

When I first got here I told the first sergeant I

wanted to go to Viet Nam. Something must have told him I shouldn't be sent there because he effectively whittled me down to size by destroying every reason (all feeble) I could bring up. Of course my 1049 was never considered.

Maybe I wanted to go because it was the easiest and most romantic thing to do. I still want to go, but for different, harder reasons.

Although I think the U.S. is like an overgrown man afraid to death of using his strength because he might kill someone, and I think the U.S. should be more forceful with the V.C. and China, I basically believe in our commitment there. Sure the war is criminal and illegal, like some 'cruit recently jailed at Ft. Dix said it is, but what war has ever been non-criminal and perfectly legal? The thing that should govern the U.S.'s war policy is whether the war is necessary or not, not whether it is criminal and illegal or not; because it is the latter that is obvious and only the former that is debatable.

Because China is a big crazy aggressive country, I believe that all of Southeast Asia (and perhaps more) will be involved in a major war within the next few years. To me, Viet Nam is just a prelude to the conflict to come. That the U.S. will be involved in the next conflict can be taken for granted; she cannot afford not to be.

So I want to go to Viet Nam not just for the sake of South Viet Nam, but for the sake of all the free nations there and everywhere.

I don't feel like some other Americans do about Viet Nam. Those who I am talking about cannot or will not see the full implications of what is taking place there. Perhaps the thing that they need to change their views is another incident like Pearl Harbor. But maybe this sounds too farfetched to them. Maybe they will be less disturbed by the mere conquest of India and Malaysia followed by Japan and possibly Australia. If they cannot find this credible, what in the hell do they think Red aggression in Korea and Viet Nam was and is all about?

Dad, what you saw in Poland I see in Viet Nam. Whether or not I go remains to be seen.

The leaves are golden and falling. Mornings are crisp and misty now, and soon it will be cold.

If you want, you can tell Mom how I feel about Viet Nam, but don't tell her that I'm trying to go there. If my 1049 is approved, it won't be for 3 or more months, anyhow. I will get a long leave in the U.S. before I would go.

I guess I've been running off at the mouth a little, so I'll sign off.

Love, Scott

11 Nov 66

Hello everybody!

Well, I guess I'll start off by thanking you for the birthday envelope. The cards, pictures, etc. were appreciated. The $ went for a new watch and the Peanuts book was great. Actually, I don't know why I put off buying a new watch for so long. My old watch busted before I came in the Army—nearly 10 months ago--*wow*--and I got used to not having one. But I have a new one now and you to thank for it.

I supposed it's been a while since I've written—but not much has been happening.

The 10-day field problem of last month went OK. Enclosed is a picture of myself and Pete Sartino of Birmingham Ala—while working on a short cable line. The photo appeared in the 8th Division's newspaper.

Today I went and bought 2 prs. of pants and 2 shirts and a pr. of shoes.

Got a letter from Clyde the other day. I don't know what kind of stuff he writes to you, but his letters to me are lousy. Actually, his letter wasn't <u>that</u> bad, but the expectations far exceeded the actual event.

You all probably remember Jim Baxter, the Io-
wan who I knew in basic and AIT. We were supposed to
go to jump school together, but his orders got fouled up
and he went to Arizona. I got a letter from him a couple
weeks ago to find he ended up in Viet Nam. He's with
the 459th Signal Battalion. He had some interesting
things to say about the place—and if I hadn't volunteered
before I got his letter, I certainly would have after. The
motivating factor being that he is risking his life and ac-
complishing something in Viet Nam and that I am going
stir crazy by spending 8 worthless hours a day in A Company's motor pool pulling "maintenance" on my truck. I
really feel useless over here, which prompts me to:

A SHORT TREATISE ON:
RUSSIAN STRATEGY IN EUROPE: THE UN-
NECESSARY CRIMP ON W. GERMANY'S ARMY;
TWO EVENTS WHICH OUTMODE U.S.-EUROPEAN
POLICYS & ARMS AGREEMENTS: THE RELATION
OF THE THREE ABOVE ITEMS: AND A THREE
STEP PLAN TO MAKE EVERYONE INVOLVED
HAPPY AND YET MAINTAIN A STRONG DEFENCE
AGAINST THE SPREAD OF COMMUNISM:

First of all, I'll admit that the Russians are out to
"bury us." They have said as much and I have no reason
to doubt this to be their intention. In my mind there is no
doubt that there is a Red threat, in Europe especially because of the proximity of Red borders. Since we know
their intentions, which is to overcome the free world, all
that is left is to discover their methods. A decimated
population and a devastated countryside, besides damage
done to their own country, would not fulfill their require-
ments for takeover of a foreign country like, say, West
Germany. So an all out military assault risking U.S. involvement is impracticable. Sabotage and other subversive
methods are out because this would only harden their prey

against Communism. Guerilla warfare like in Mao's Phase I would not work in this type of country, an open terrain easily defendable against such attack. The best method would be to try and take over the government thru election of pro-communist people. The easiest way to get these people elected is either by concealment of their real intentions, or by creating economic unrest, paving the way for someone new. I believe this method, or some variation thereof, to be the method the Communists will use and currently are using. Of course, a military coup would be feasible, but as long as the army is kept strong and pro Western, and the economy is kept stable, this is unlikely. A strong and well equipped military is still needed, despite the fact that the Reds will probably use more peaceful methods to take over. The main reason for this is that if the country didn't maintain a strong army, the Russians could simply move in and take over by force.

So a major military force is still necessary. The West Germans could support an army of a million men, yet post WWII agreements limit them to 500,000. The crimp on the size of the West German army stems from the world's fear that the Germans will rise again and try to conquer the world. But with the country half its former size, or nearly so, and the fact that the country is pro West, makes this possibility very remote. Why not let the West Germans assume total responsibility for their national defense? This would free the U.S., France and England from maintaining a total of 365,000 troops in Germany. Certainly the Germans could make up for its allied forces; military experts and German generals both agree the country could support 500,000 additional men, let alone 365,000. This crimp on the German army is unneeded and should be ended, or at least loosened.

The U.S. –European defense agreements need not be ended entirely—with the possible withdrawal of U.S. troops. This is definitely not what the U.S. wants. We are interested in the defense of Europe for our own good as well as Europe's. There are two things the U.S. has done since WWII that would make a physically non-present involvement possible. One, the ICBM[2] and SAC[3]; two, the U.S. ability to move great numbers of troops and equipment in a short time across the ocean. The ICBM and SAC could deliver devastating blows to whomever we want wherever we want. As far as an actual troop commitment, the U.S. did show in 1962 that it has the airpower to move whole divisions to Europe in several days. These two developments could be used to great advantage in a revision of U.S. foreign policy.

Such revisions would solve the problem of difficult German purchasing of U.S. military goods that they would rather produce themselves, but are bound to buy because of a balance of payment agreement between the U.S. and Germany. The withdrawal of foreign troops, tho friendly, would cease "litterbugging" and help the county toward constructive national identity. With bringing the 225,000 U.S. troops home, the U.S. would have substantially reduced the gold flow and cut down the expense of maintaining such a force so far away from the U.S. Not only that, but the U.S. would have released just that many men for duty in other troubled parts of the world—like Viet Nam.

An allied troop withdrawal from West Germany would be beneficial for all concerned. Financially it would help the Germans and its allies, and if a strong military alliance is kept between the nations, the Red threat would still be curbed. Other non-tangible results would be a revival of strong national identity within Germany, and, perhaps of lesser concern, the knowledge that would arise in one, Scott Christofferson's heart—that he is not a litterbug.

At the same time these troops are withdrawn

---

[2] *Intercontinental Ballistic Missile*
[3] *Strategic air command*

other things must be done. One, the Germans should be
allowed to develop nuclear capabilities. The idea of a U.S.
monopoly on it is unreasonable. Two, the Germans
should be allowed to enlarge their army enough to fulfill
their defense needs. And three, the U.S. should make a
simple statement of a new U.S. –European policy. The
policy should say that the U.S. is determined to prevent
the spread of Communism in Europe and will combat to
the fullest extent attack on any free country in Europe by
Russia or its satellites.

End of essay.

After reading this essay I wrote, I have come to
the conclusion that I don't feel useless here, it's just that
I'd rather be elsewhere. I suppose I just want to be more
physically involved with the containment of Communism.
And not to be a litterbug in such a beautiful country as
this.

Actually, the more I see of our men and what
they do, the more I think we should go back to where we
came from.

12 Nov 66

Well, I guess I'll mail this now or else it will
never get to you.

Scott

Hi folks —   25/11/66

that for variation, I'd send
a postcard. The river on the
picture is the Nahe. The
structure on the hill is what
used to be a castle - now a
ruinous thing. Walls on hillside
remenants of city wall.
Received Jim, Peter and
Frank's too. Frank's drawing
was great. Got a letter from
the Lautman's.

(Haven't been writing)(seems
thing have settled into an abyss
of boredom and is little to
write about. However, will
endeavor to create an epic
letter
mid-December. However, don't expect much.

                    Scott

C.amers Kunstanstalt KG, Dortmund

AIRMAIL

Christoffersons
3 Thorndell
St. Louis, 17, Missouri

28 NOV 1966

U.S. AIRMAIL 8¢

Dec. '66

Dear Dad,
      I received your letter and magazine clippings.
That "Fortune" article on rising nationalism in Europe was
a well written and astute commentary on contemporary
Europe. After reading that, and considering what is pres-
ently going on in West Germany, I am more sure than
ever that the U.S. needs to change its foreign policy towards Europe. A different military pact is necessary and
U.S. troop withdrawal is inevitable, if the U.S. is to remain
on good terms with Western Europe. I see these things
happening in the near future, hastened by the change over
of power in Bonn. An interesting development in German
politics is the present popularity of the NPD, a neo-Nazi
party, popular mainly in Bavaria. I do not see the party as
the resurrection of Nazism,as many do, but as the somewhat misled result of German nationalism. I back this up
with the fact that the main goals of the party are (1) that
the U.S. withdraw its troops and (2) that W. Germany
gain nuclear power for its defense and (3) the reunification
of Germany. Although the movement is in somewhat
dangerous hands (racism and light degrees of terrorism
are in evidence), I am sure as a whole the German population does not want Nazism again and will maintain a
strong alliance with the U.S. I am sure the party will be
molded by the German people into a healthy instrument
of Nationalism. I am equally confident that the German
people will destroy the party if it proves to be a tool of
Nazism and cannot be molded.
      Enough of that.
      I got a letter from Mrs. Lautman the other day. I
hope they get here before I leave.
      It's been nearly 11 months since I joined the
Army and I think I can look back now and analyze things
fairly well. Analyze, mainly, the reason I left college; the
reason I joined the Army; and some results thereof.

It might be easier to determine why I quit school by first saying why I didn't quit school. That is, to list some reasons you or other people may have that aren't valid reasons. These are: unrequited love; desire to get out of the house; lack of desire to complete school; inability to adjust to college life; excessive mental instability; or the unconscious fulfillment of a youthful decision. Now that I've stated why I *didn't* leave school, I'll tell you why I *did* leave school. A break of several years from high school to college would (1) enable me to go into college no longer a minor (this entails several things: a 21 older can own a car and live off campus, two things I want to be able to do when I go to college); (2) allow me ample time to get an idea of what I want to do in life and in college; (an 18 year older in the insulated lap of luxury can have few serious goals as opposed to a 21 year older who's been exposed to things for 3 years). (3) Another reason, a little less definable than the others, is that I was confused about myself and things around me and I felt the need to radically change my environment. Perhaps by using the word "confused," I have understated the importance of this factor in my decision, but this in only for lack of a better word. I'm not too sure what constituted this confusion. It was not any one thing, but rather a combination of many colliding emotions and experiences. I found in college something that somehow eluded me on my trip to Canada, and this was the awakening of a youth to the world of reality. To some fellas I know this comes easily and naturally with no mental stress. For me, it wasn't. The cause behind this interests me (for I want it to be easier for my children) and is probably of interest to you (because I am your son and you have 5 other children who will someday face reality, too). Actually, there are 2 steps to adulthood: the facing of reality, and *how* one faces it. To my way of thinking, it is extremely important to have a healthy, normal, educated outlook. Unless I am mistaken, it is obtaining this outlook that growing up is all about. A mature person is one with a healthy outlook towards life, which implies two steps towards maturity. (1) *Seeing* life as it is and (2) *reacting* to it in a normal manner and achieving a well adjusted outlook upon it.

Unless one sees life as it is, he of course cannot react to it. Unless one has a proper development (development being in what manner a child is raised—fears, anxiety, obsessions and all that other psychological stuff having an effect on a child's development), one might react with great difficulty and have a difficult time adjusting to life. Altho I might venture to speculate that this is where Jan is having her trouble, I will refrain because I honestly don't know enough about her or psychology. So I will keep my analysis to myself.

First of all, before I go into observations on my own case, I'd like to tell you that I'm doing this to (1) help straighten things out in my own mind and (2) to possibly provide some insight for you as to why and how I am reacting to life. Perhaps some of my observations on my own experiences can be of use to you in relation to other people in the family.

If there was any definable point where I started to see reality (the adult world as opposed to a child or youth's) it would be when I got home from Canada, summer '65. Why this process was so long in getting started I can't honestly say—I don't know. Why I reacted differently at this time to things I'd obviously seen before, again I can't say. But the point is that at this time for the first time, I perceived that you and mom were having trouble in your marriage. Ironically, this was the exact same moment that Jan found out the same thing. For her, this was another complicating factor and another step towards her eventual breakdown. For me, it was just the beginning of my awakening from a "slumber of innocence." The event itself and its implications are unimportant in a practical sense because I am now removed physically from the situation and from what I now know, the problem has been resolved, or nearly so. The incident is no longer important: what it symbolized and the process it initiated, is important. The process being my awakening to the coarser facets of life. At college other incidents occurred which hastened this process. Emotionally speaking, that semester at Mizzou was hell for me, because all at once I was being bombarded with the facts of life. It was almost funny (now) that for 18 years I'd been a child and here I was in college, an institution requiring adulthood, and I was just then going through adolescence. (Or whatever the hell they call it when you find out that life has its ugly sides.) Of course seeing and reacting don't happen too far apart—they're simultaneous. I was reacting all the time—which explains the dilemmas and strains I faced at the time. Things reached a frenzied height just a couple weeks before finals and, unable to make sense out of anything, I eased my tensions by drinking. This lasted for about a week and a half until I suddenly realized that I had best catch hold of myself or I'd be in real trouble. I had decided almost at the onset of college that with this turmoil within me I was not prepared for college and should quit, and at this time I was more sure than ever that I should leave school. Perhaps this best describes just why I left school

After flying off on a wild tangent for 5 pages on the psychology behind why I quit school, I will continue with the main purpose of this letter as stated on page 3, paragraph 3. But first I'll say that after joining the Army I began to see things in a more normal light and now, almost 11 months later, I am pretty well settled, emotionally speaking.

Why I joined the Army. Well, it was pretty obvious I couldn't continue in any school, so going to U. of Mo. or another was out. I suppose I could have gotten a job, but the draft would have gotten me before long. And besides, I don't think I could have conveyed to you what was going on in my mind. The Army presented itself as the most practical thing to do, and that's why I joined it.

Some results of what I've done in the last 11 months: I've reached a normal emotional outlook. I'm getting my military obligation behind me. And I've pretty much found myself. A totally irrelevant fact but one that will put your mind to rest about my future, is that I hate the Army and really look forward to getting out. I plan on living a long, normal life –outside the Army. The Army is a miserable organization and 3 years in it will be more than enough.

16 Dec. '66

Well I let this letter ferment for 12 days and then reread it to see if I'd still want to send it.

You'll die when you hear what the Lautman's sent me. "How to See Europe on $5 A Day," enclosed with a 20 dm bill—according to current exchange, 20 marks is 5 dollars.

Grandma Ursula sent me a card and so did Grandma Helen.

Today I got a card from Jan. She sounds great. From her note I'm reassured she'll be all right.

I got a letter from Mom the other day—it was good to hear from her.

A couple of things I wrote down on a scratch paper to remember to tell you, but don't exactly fit into the rest of the letter:

I've been saving about 20% of my income. So far I've made slightly over a thousand dollars and have saved $225. This isn't a heck of a lot, but it'll add up and when I get out I'll be able to buy a car and go back to college.

As far as my 1049 to Viet Nam is concerned, I should hear from them any week now.

25 Dec. '66

Well this letter is taking longer than I thot to finish.

The last couple of weeks have been especially

pleasant for me. We haven't been working much because of Christmas and I've had lots of time to read, write and just think and enjoy things.

The thinking and reflection I've been doing has been slow, deep and completely delightful. I've been reading novels, philosophy and poetry. Libraries are a very important thing because they are a means of communication with some very great minds. I have been learning much. Yesterday, for example, I had a very long argument with John Steinbeck (*East of Eden*, 539 pages). We argued on points of religion, philosophy and man's basic nature. Actually it wasn't much of a debate. He effectively, efficiently and completely overwhelmed me. Against his well presented points I would bring up only feeble and poorly made protests. I have found out that I have a very small mind and I would do better to just listen to those minds greater. The other day Robert Frost made a fool of me. Dylan Thomas has made me see things I never before knew existed. Last week Carl Sandburg rubbed my nose in my own ignorance and littleness.

My personal beliefs have been torn down and ridiculed. I am back in kindergarten. But I am optimistic, for I have good teachers. The first lesson I have learned in my re-education is a great respect for the human soul. This is something all my new teachers have impressed upon me. To me this sounds like a firm basis for education: Does it to you?

The purpose behind this letter is to let you know what kind of a person I am becoming. I think it important for a father to know his son. Likewise I think a son should know his father. There are many things I would like to say to you and ask of you, but I can't in a letter. You don't know how much I look forward to coming home and seeing you and talking to you. I'm not sure what caused me to build a barrier between us but I will do my best to tear it down.

This letter has been three weeks in the making

and if I don't mail it now I'm afraid it never will get mailed.

Oh—a few final messages.

I got a card from Miss Rains, and a box of cookies from the Lautmans. I heard they lost the contract and won't be coming here.

The envelope from home mom told me about hasn't come yet but I await it eagerly.

Say hi to the family for me. Happy New Year's.

Scott

28 December 66

Dear Mr. Carnahan—

As you can guess, my handwriting hasn't improved so I still print.

I greatly appreciated your letter and especially the snapshots. They will give me a much desired opportunity to meet some German people on a social basis—a thing that is somewhat difficult for a G.I. in Germany.

I have been the dubious driver of a monstrous deuce and a half thru Mainz several times. That town is a mere 10-12 miles up the road from Bad Krueznach, where I am stationed. Can the Siebens⁵ speak English? I'm afraid I haven't picked up much German, so a language problem might occur. Up till now, the only German phrases I have found necessary have been "Eine bier" (accompanied with an upright thumb, not one finger as in the states) and "Dunka."

Your advice to "space your drinks" (which you gave me previously) fell the way of most advice from one generation to another, I'm afraid. On one such occasion I made a long distance phone call from North Augusta, just

---

⁴*Mr. Carnachan had put Scott in touch with the Siebens , a family he knew in Germany*

across the river into South Carolina, to my home in St. Louis. It was on the evening of my departure to Ft. Benning for Airborne School and cost quite a bit. Actually, I think I was sober enough for the call to be appreciated, but from then on I have made sure there is no phone nearby when I sit down to drink. Several times since then I have wakened up with the phrase, "Remember! Space your drinks!" being repeated over and over again in my reeling head, myself understanding the truth in the statement as I stagger to the latrine, sick and about to vomit.

As I look back at it now I can more accurately say why I quit school than I could then. Simply, my young soul was being bombarded with the facts of life and I decided because I could not and did not want to study, that I should leave school. At the time I made all kinds of excuses but they were wrong. I quit because my mind was in a chaotic state. Why it took 18 years to see some of the coarser sides of life, I don't know. Perhaps I saw them before but refused to recognize them for what they stood for. How come I reacted in such a way to cause the confusion I felt then, I don't know. At this time, 11 months later, I can say that this particular confusion no longer exists. However, there is always one confusion to replace another, but happily I react to them in a more mature way than before.

I had to leave school. And I wanted independence. I felt a need to see Viet Nam. The Army was the best thing, so without telling my parents, I went and enlisted.

Immediately I was put in a position of leadership. For reasons unknown to myself, I was sent to a Leaders Orientation School, which lasted for a week. I emerged exactly the way I went in. I didn't feel one damn bit more of a Leader, but I had acting buck sergeant's stripes and was sent to a basic training company. There are two of these creatures with phony rank in each platoon. Generally these people are despised because they are just the

89

same as the rest of the 'cruits but have rank over them.

The main purpose behind having us "acting jacks" is to take some of the load off the <u>real</u> sergeants. Apparently because of the buildup, there is a lack of Drill Instructors so they are spread a bit thin. Our task was simply to make sure the barracks were kept spotless and to aid in training with the fundamentals taught us in LOC school.

For some reason myself, and the other acting sgt., Bob Curley, escaped the typical hatred of acting jacks. In fact, the men liked us and we ended up with the best platoon in the company. I won a trophy for physical training at the end of basic, and was promoted to E-Z and thus ended my first phase of training well.

Altho I had enlisted for Airborne Infantry I was sent to Wireman school. After 4 weeks at Ft. Leonard Wood (this was after 13 days leave), I was sent to Ft. Gordon, Georgia, for 6 more weeks of Lineman School. That was at the end of May.

After I graduated from Lineman School July 8th, I got orders to Ft. Benning for Airborne School. And that was the hardest 3 weeks I ever spent. The first two weeks were contained of intense physical conditioning as well as classes and practicing in the procedures and methods of preparing to jump, exiting the aircraft, and hitting the ground. In the third week we made a total of 5 jumps from a C-119 at 1250 ft. It was great fun.

So, "with silver wings upon my chest" I awaited my orders to Viet Nam. I was sure that's where they would send me because I volunteered for it. I got orders to Germany. We flew to New York and boarded the SS Rose. That 9 days at sea was fun. Great weather and, because I did my best to dodge them, no details. I read a lot on the sunny deck and thoroughly enjoyed myself. We got to Bremerhaven on the 10th of August. I thot I'd be assigned to the 509th Airborne but wasn't. They sent me to the 8th Signal Battalion.

After about 3 months I couldn't stand it any longer and put in a form 1049 for Viet Nam. This was at the end of October. If I am not sent by late January, I will either put in another 1049 or write the President and ask him if he wants to win the war or not. I think my desire to go to Viet Nam is being thwarted by Communists who have infiltrated our higher command. Of course I'm joking but I think it odd that I haven't been sent. Mom thinks it funny I haven't been sent yet—but I can tell she's happy because of it.

Why do I want to go to Viet Nam? A little bit of patriotism. A little bit because I honestly believe the Chinese are dangerous and must be contained—better in Viet Nam than in India, Japan or Australia. But mostly because I want to see firsthand the tragic results of man's failure as a thinking being. This last reason is probably foolish—because a person like yourself could tell me exactly what it's like—but I'll do it for the same reason I failed to heed the advice "Remember! Space your drinks!" But none of your wisdom is wasted.

In the next installment expect a critical essay on the poetry of Dylan Thomas; "East of Eden"; and how I feel about the world today; and a ridiculous essay on man.

Scott.

6 Jan 67

Hello everybody—

If you had anything insurable in that Christmas envelope—you'd better notify Lloyd's and have them pay you off. It never got here. Maybe it was just misaddressed and is slowly finding its way —as of now it hasn't come.

I got mom's letters and also one from Carrie.

Too bad Uncle Les' company didn't get the contract. They are missing out on what could have been a great experience.

91

Of course I was sad to hear about Uncle Bud[5].

Roger Becker joined the Army last Sept. He enlisted for 4 years and hopes to go OCS. Now he's in Monterey, Calif. for a 37 week Russian course.

I will be making Spec 4 this month—around the 18th. Rumors of a flock of orders for V.N. are swirling around—with usual frequency and validity. If they don't come down this month I'll just put in for it again. If so, I'll take a leave in Feb. or March and see some of the country.

Tomorrow is an 8th div. holiday because of an anniversary of the div.'s birthday. So I'll go up to Mainz and see the Seibens to return for Mr. Carnachan some photos. The train will get me there in about ½ hour. Mainz is only 40 km up the road. (22 or so miles.) This will be a good opportunity to meet some Germans on a social basis—something I haven't been able to do yet.

In 18 days I'll have only 1,051,200 minutes to go.

Scott

23 Jan 67

Hi Clyde—

Seldom, yes. But when you write it's one hell of a letter. That 21-page epic was magnificent. No shit. It was great. I don't expect to hear from you again for many months.

The description of the house and the characterizations of Carl and Jim made me feel like I haven't been away for long at all. Eight months tomorrow since I saw any Christoffersons. Doesn't seem that long. And more than a year since I've seen you. Tempus sure fugits.

The part of your letter about Viet Nam was real good. I had been struggling with <u>Background—Viet Nam</u> by Bernard Newman, mostly to find some more rea-

---

[5] *Scott's uncle John "Bud" Lavach was killed in a car accident December 23, 1966*

sons for risking my fool neck there, and after reading your
letter I threw the book away. What you said makes real
sense. It is an interesting question—can and /or should
Communist factions be represented in a Democratic government? I agree with you that a Communist-Democratic
government would probably not survive. Like you said,
any faction that wants to take over the power making
process will screw up the works. I think you were correct
in implying that it is not against the principles of a Democratic system to outlaw factions bent on destroying the
system.

Are the nationalists in Viet Nam a minority? Are
the Communists the majority? Do the possibly minority
nationalists survive only by U.S. presence? The nationalists probably do survive only because of the U.S.; if so, and
if the nationalists are a minority, should the U.S. support
the military? It may seem that these are the questions to
be asked and answered in relation to U.S. involvement in
Viet Nam—or any Communist-free front—but are they?

Like Steinbeck (East of Eden—in my last letter I
think I referred to it) says, the factor that makes man
great is his ability to choose. Without this intellectual
ability, man is nothing exceptional. It seems to me that
this ability to choose is man's right. Hell, it's his only
unique characteristic—it better be his right to have it.
Does a bird have to earn or deserve his right to fly? Hell
no. He was born with wings—and he was also born with
the right to use them. So with man; he was born with his
ability to choose plus the right to choose. He doesn't have
to ask permission to use it—neither need he thank anyone
for it.

To deny man the right to choose is an incredible
bit of presumptuousness. (sp? Right word?) Man realizes
this perversity and resists it. He has always rebelled
against physical or intellectual restrictions on this right to
choose, and if he ever stops rebelling, then man has had it.

Perhaps the Reds in Viet Nam should be opposed

because of the infringements they employ on men—not whether or not the Communists are a minority or a majority, or whatever. We should oppose the Communists—or any like organization—simply because they are out to destroy man's single engreatening factor. This is the life-and-death struggle of man's birthrights. (And after all, what else do we have?)

The question arises: If man chooses to yield this right—then what?

I'm not sure I can answer this. But there are certain points to be considered in attempting to.

Has man ever done this? No, I don't think so. To a certain extent—to matters of economics, politics and some other things, yes. But to a total degree? No.

Is man capable of doing this voluntarily? No, no more than a bird is capable of not flying.

Can man ever be manipulated and mutilated to such an extent where he would do such a thing? A bird could be hurt so he couldn't fly. Perhaps man could, too. But I doubt it. The analogy is weak on this point because of the complexity of man's nature. Maybe he could and maybe he couldn't—but I don't want to find out. So I'll oppress any attempt to deform or limit man's basic nature out of sheer self preservation

That was deeper than I intended to go. I'd like to know your opinions on this, tho. (In the Army, one seldom meets anyone who thinks. Either they don't exist or the atmosphere is so stifling to such activity that they might as well not.)

My reading and writing (mostly free verse, prose and some abominable poetry) is just about my only intellectual outlet. Carrying on a monologue is frustrating—and rather depressing as well.

Another outlet stifled because of the army is the boy-girl emotional relationship. You can't conceive how God damn happy I'll be to get out and carry on a normal relationship with a girl.

Outside of these two, the other basic needs are readily taken care of. Whores in Frankfurt gobble up much G.I. dollars. Athletic activity is easy to come by. Movies and bars take care of escapism.

Yes. Between prostitutes, the shows and booze, the G.I.'s paycheck is taken care of pretty quickly.

This is probably the grimiest picture I've ever drawn of the Army. But it is an accurate one. The Army sucks. Enough of that.

The other day I got a postcard from the Department of the Army. They said they got my request for reassignment to Viet Nam. I can't see any reason for them turning me down, so I should get my orders soon. And I'll be glad to leave here—a peace time Army is the most useless and stupid thing in the Universe. A soldier should fight and if he doesn't he should be made into a civilian.

I just read Elia Kazan's America, America. I'm not sure I like what he said—but I like how he said it. Hemingway's The Sun Also Rises was really good. The more I read by him the better I like him

Mr. Carnachan sent me the address of a family he knows in Mainz. They are German and apparently after the war they received "care" type packages from Mr. Carnachan. I don't know if Mr. Carnachan knew the Siebens before that, but they were so grateful they made Mr. Carnachan a godfather of a daughter born shortly after the war (by proxy).

Mainz is 40 klicks up the road. By train, it took me about a half hour. It is a big town—130,000 people. Eighty percent of it was destroyed during the War, and things were very harsh when they received the packages of food and clothing.

Hermut Something and his brother, now 27 and 25 respectively, were taken in by Dr. Sieben after the War. I think both or one of their parents died in the War. Hermut is now a priest in Russelshiem and his brother is a construction engineer in Malaw, S. Africa. Hermut speaks

English fairly well. He's a good guy—offered me the use of his VW and told me he'd come to B.K. some time to see me. The Sunday I was in Mainz, Hermut and myself, plus Robert and Clause Sieben went sledding at a winter resort area. Robert is about 14 and Claus 10. Strong, healthy young kids. After sledding we returned to the Siebens and had dinner. Potatoes, different types of meat chopped up and skewered on a small stick, and carrots. Eating on plates and drinking out of glasses is a rare luxury for a G.I. Wine was served with the meal. Dr. Sieben is an elderly, educated man. He reads English better than he speaks but we communicated fairly well. Mrs. Sieben is a quick and interesting lady. She made me feel real at ease. I was seated next to Carnachan's god-daughter, Barbara. She is 17 and fragile and very good looking. If I weren't a scum-sucking G.I. who will probably leave Germany soon, I'd really like to pursue things with her. She was reserved and demure—but by no means a wall-flower type. She had her mother's quick wit and was charming. Fidela (11 or 12) was Barbara's duplicate—just smaller. She was shy but all smiles. Another daughter is 15 and in France studying—I guess, to be a nun. They invited me back and maybe when I can I will go.

I'm writing this from the Service Club. It is a two story building containing a pool hall, library, craft-shop, music room and the living room where I'm sitting. Plays and USO shows appear in this room on a built-in stage. The second story rear windows overlook the motor pool. All of the 200 or so Signal Battalion trucks are in the motor pool, along with a motor shop for each of the 3 companies. The motor pool is shaped like a backwards L and surrounds the Service Club from the rear and side. A high barbed wire fence encloses the motor pool which is about 6 football field lengths in its inner length and perhaps 50 yards across. Most of the trucks are deuce and a half's but there are many ¾'s and jeeps. In "A" Company, the length of trucks closest to the Service Club, there are basically 3 types of trucks. Deuce and a half's with VHF vans on their beds, or switchboard or radio vans; ¾'s with much smaller vans—radio, patch panels, teletype etc. etc.; and trucks with all the assorted material and supplies the battalion needs—cable, wire, tents, etc. etc. Most of the trucks and vans on them pull trailers with generators in them. These generators supply the power needed for communication, heat, lights. I drive A-152, a deuce and a half with about 92 reels of 26 pair cable in it. I am a "wire rat" or "cable dog." On field problems we string cable thru trees between VHF rigs and patch panels (patch panels "patch" VHF to teletype to radio) between patch panels and switchboards. We string field wire to generals' vans, mess halls and any place else our sergeants think of for direct telephone communication. Once I installed a telephone in a one-star general's van. It was mounted on the back of a deuce ½ and had wall to wall carpeting, antiqued birch walls (or mahogany—I don't know a lot about wood) a bed, a desk, a closet, and get this—a porcelain urinal on a wall next to the closet, plus a commode in another closet. These guys have really got it good.

We haven't had a big field problem since October. This month we had a 3 day exercise, tho, and next month a big 10-11 day problem is scheduled. I hope I get my orders soon because I don't relish going out in the cold for 10 days.

Beyond the motor pool is a track, football field, two baseball fields and a barbed wire fence. Beyond the fence is a cluster of German Apartment houses.

A –Signal & MP billets & mess hall

B – Service Club—also a barber shop, tailors, snack bar, gym, etc.

C – Motor pool

D – EM Club –booze and band and occasionally go-go girls.

E – Theatre

That is somewhat how the part of the concern

which contains the 8th Signal looks. This shows only half the entire concern—there is the 8th Inf. Div. Headquarters, 708th maintenance, 8th division band, post office, and a lot of other buildings here. A bowling alley, NCO Club, and an indoor rifle range are also on post. I guess there are a couple thousand men here.

The post is towards the outskirts of B.K. (Bad Krueznach). It is 30,000 and basically a G.I. town. There are lots of bars downtown and plenty of girls to sucker your money. The first time I went downtown I spent around 25 dollars on some fat ugly bitch—whose good looks increased in direct proportion to the amount of booze I consumed. It hasn't happened to me since, tho. The girls downtown lead you on but it's hard to get them into bed. They usually get you to buy them drinks. They dance with you and pat your dick to get you to do this. I usually get so pissed off downtown that I don't go down there very much.

"A" Co. has 3 platoons. I'm in first platoon. There are 3 sections in first platoon, 10-15 men per section. Wire section (my section), VHF section, and radio section. Second platoon is the same. Third platoon is comm.-center and Headquarters.

Our barracks are drab looking 3-story structures. Like all the rest of the buildings on post, Hitler's men once lived in them. (In 1941 those men went to fight in France.)

I sleep in 1st platoon wire and VHF Bay. It is crowded. On regular work days—Mon-Fri—we spend most of our time in the Motor pool. There isn't a hell of a lot to do there, but we do it anyway. There isn't enough to keep us busy, but you have to give the appearance of occupation to get along. So I just walk around my truck, a wrench in one hand and a screw driver in the other, looking like I'm doing something. Being in the motor pool is boring as hell. Saturdays are for inspection—arms, wall locker and footlocker; TA-150 (field equipment-personal); truck inspections. All are senseless and only to kill time, I think. At 12:00 on Sat., we are usually let off. Sundays are off.

A typical day:

6:00 –the CQ (Charge of Quarters) starts waking everybody up. This is absolutely the worst time of day. The Son-of-a-bitch blows a whistle loud as hell—it's a horrible way to get up. Grumbling and cursing, we get up.

By 6:25 we are dressed. Another whistle then gets us outside in company formation. A big colored staff sgt. waits for everyone to fall in. It is dark and usually very cold.

"Fall in!" he booms. He has a loud voice and we call him the obvious nickname—"Foghorn." He is a gung-ho SOB and we don't like him very much. Another nickname he has is "Smoke." This is because he is constantly bringing smoke on our asses: An Army phrase meaning that he is a pee-bringer: Another Army phrase that means he is constantly yelling at us about mox-nix stuff. He and his kind are disdainfully referred to as "life sons of bitches." (Lifer—career soldier.)

Then he says, "Report."

The platoon sgts., one at a time, salute and give their reports.

After that he booms, "Left…"

(The platoon sgts. repeat his command.)

"Face!" We all turn to our left in a half assed manner. Our morale is very low. This is a very bad time of day for all of us. It is dark, cold, we are tired, and probably suffering from a hang-over.

He then booms, "Forward……" (by the way, all this "booming" Foghorn does is unpleasant to our ears at this tender time of day. I think I hate the Army most at this time.

"March."

We then march out to the road where the entire

Signal Battalion congregates for the pagan custom known as reveille.

This is a totally ridiculous thing. A man—his body somewhere out there in the dark—yells, "Battal—ion!" The Company sgts. repeat the preparatory command—"Company!" booms Foghorn.

"Atten----shut!"

We bring our feet together. All the snap and crackle of basic training is gone. You hear the breathing of the men and smell the stale smell of booze drunk the night before.

"PRESENT!" screams the bodiless voice. (The company sgts. repeat the command.)

"H'arms!"

We haphazardly lift our arms and salute. Exactly what we are saluting, I don't know: because we are facing the mess hall and not a flag. Even if a flag was there, we wouldn't be able to see it. The sun hasn't even peeked over the hills to the East yet, and it won't for another hour.

After several seconds,

"Order!...." again the Voice. (Foghorn repeats in a thunderous voice, "Order!")

"H'arms! Company sergeants take charge of your men and release them for chow."

"Fall out for chow!" Like a cannon.

Some of us drift over to the mess hall. Others go to our bay and start cleaning up the place.

It is now 7:45, everyone has eaten chow, the barracks are swept, mopped and dusted. Another whistle. We put on our hats, coats and gloves and wander out into a company formation. It is now fairly light, altho we can't see the sun.

The first sgt. comes out before the company. There is another report. The first sgt. is a Vietnam vet, 15 years in the service, and a pretty good man.

He says (in the tone of a recorded announcement):

"Platoon sergeants take your men out on police call and form them up here at" (he looks mechanically at his watch) "at 0755." Salutes.

After police call he again faces the company. He has been talking for several minutes, bits and snatches of the announcements reaching your ears. I think it is the exact same speech every day.

"The billets....like a whorehouse!"

"And the next time...beer bottles...will be an article 15."

"There will be.....no more....this....that... yukkity....yak."

Later we march over to the motor pool. After four hours of nothing we march back for mail call and chow. Then we return to the motor pool (sometimes referred to as "cess"pool) for another 4 hours. At 5:00 (1700) we are subjugated to another speech like the one in the morning, threatened with a G.I. party the next time the barracks look so bad---and finally released.

Chow is served at 5:30 – 6:30. The flick starts at 6:30 and 8:30. You get showered, dressed, eat, go to the show, stop by at the EM club for a drink or two, come back to the billets, shoot a game of pool, get undressed, read some or write some, and go to sleep, are awakened 4 or 5 times by loud drunks coming in during the night and at 6:00 that god-damn whistle wakes you up again. It's a ball.

Some other goodies of Army life in Europe are: once a month shakedown inspection and alerts. These shakedowns reaffirm my conviction that the Army authorized Democracy only for civilians. At about 4 in the morning the lights are thrown on, whistles blown, and you are ordered to get up and unlock both your foot and wall lockers. Then some nasty sergeant rummages thru your belongings looking for god knows what. You do nothing but curse them under your breath and hope that perhaps some day you'll get a chance to run them over with a truck.

Alerts are nice too. Once or twice a month sirens will wail and no matter where you are or what you are doing, you must get in duty uniform, collect your weapon and field gear, hop in your truck and drive 5 miles out to the alert area. Usually they call one right in the middle of a movie. After several hours of sitting in your cold truck the alert is over. Drive back to the motor pool, complete your mileage and fuel consumption, clean-up your truck, and await instructions for the rest of the day. Just a random piece of information—if my diesel burning truck gets 4 miles to a gallon, I'm lucky.

I will welcome danger and possible death in Viet Nam over the stagnant existence I have here.

Remember Roger Becker? He joined the Army last September. He's now in Monterey, Calif. for Russian School. He enlisted for 4 years and plans on going to OCS.

Mom told me Becky Maxwell got married. Her married name—Becky Bopp. Wow!

(This has gotten longer than I intended.)

Scott

5 Feb 67

Hello everyone;

Right now I'm on motor pool guard. It's fairly cold out so I'm in the motor pool shack. There's a typewriter here so I'm using it.

As usual, not much has been happening. Tomorrow I'll be off and I'm going to Mainz. The Siebens invited me for the carnival and parade there. This weekend was a festival downtown. Real wild and colorful. Only a real tragedy happened when a GI ran over and killed a German last night.

My section chief and my platoon sgt. both told me that my orders will be coming down this month. They said that the First Sgt. told them, so I guess it's true. I've heard so many rumors, though. Unless I get my orders before the 16th, I'll be going out to the field. It is supposed to be another ten day problem around Fulda, near where we had one last October.

If what I hear about my orders is true, I might be home on leave pretty soon. I'd like to be able to drive while I'm home and a couple ideas have come to me about that. First, would I be able to drive under the insurance you have now? I'm pretty sure I won't, so how can I get insured real quick like? Of course any expense will be mine. Please look into this and write me about what you come up with. Second, what's the possibility of renting or leasing a car for a month or so? It should only take a couple of quick phone calls to find the answers to these questions. I'd do it myself if I could but I can't. And please let me know as soon as you can, the answer to these questions or any other solution to the insurance-car problem. There are a lot of things I would like to do on leave and I need the use of a car for them.

Clyde wrote me an unprecedented (and probably never to be equaled) twenty-one page letter a few weeks ago. He seldom writes but when he does it's a good letter. His views on Viet-Nam were well formulated and sound. He presented one of the best reasons for US involvement that I have ever heard with an analogy concerning the human body. When the body is attacked by outside diseases it generally responds to the infection with self-produced antibodies. Thus most minor illnesses are cured. However, occasionally a disease, like cancer, infects the body and the body cannot counteract it effectively. Outside help is brought in, the form being a doctor and a hospital. In the case of Viet Nam Communism from the North is the cancer and the US is the outside help. A quick look at the history of Viet Nam will show that the

103

disease <u>is</u> external in nature-thus the argument that the disease is self induced and therefore none of the US's business, is invalid.

Clyde also told me in detail the changes in the house. I'm eager to see them.

Write soon

Scott

P.S. I only have 719 days left.

Scott Christofferson
A Co 8th Signal 13n
APO New York 09111

22 Feb 67

Hi--

I'm out in the field now, and have been since 16 Feb. We're about 18 klicks from Fulda. The East German border is in sight from the hill we're on.

Winds of up to 50 knots and heavy rains have made this a muddy and unpleasant field problem. It's pretty cold, but the snow that was here when we came is gone. We're on the highest hills in the area and we have a good view of the countryside.

Right now I'm working a switchboard. Before I had been laying cable and digging holes. Tonight we'll probably tear down and tomorrow we'll move out-back to B.K. Next month we'll probably be out for two weeks.

When I went to Mainz for the festivities a few weeks ago I had a ball. It was on a Monday and to get it off I had to volunteer for duty Sat. and Sunday. Sat. I was on a trash truck and Sun. I was on guard in the Motor Pool. On Monday I took the train to Mainz. The Sieben's son who had been working in South Africa for two years, and who I hadn't met the other time I was in Mainz, is a real cool cat. He's 25 or so and real intelligent. At the parade we and two girls and a few other couples messed around the whole day—following the floats and just being part of the fun. And was it wild! Thousands of people, all dressed in crazy costumes; dozens of marching bands and elaborate floats; beer and wine sold at every corner; the streets flooded with humanity: noise, singing and music filling the air, confetti and balloons everywhere; everything a big crazy swirl of color, noise and people. Everyone was happy and friendly. Everyone shouting greetings at everyone else. The costumed men on the floats threw candy and fruit to the people who lined the streets, and they scrambled for the gifts. People in buildings opened their windows and shouted and threw confetti to those below. It was an insane, good natured mob of people in Mainz that day. I heard it is the biggest festival in this part of Germany—and at the train station were hundreds of people—from all parts of Germany.

Sun. 26 Feb 66

We've been back from the field for several days now. The day we got back from the field the company clerk had me fill out a form telling where I would be on leave. Apparently my orders will be down in April.

I'll take a leave in March. Maybe I'll go to Spain. Me acuerdo alguno Espanol. ("I still remember some Spanish.")

The March field problem won't involve me, so I'll probably get my leave approval.

Thursday 2 March

I put in for a 7 day leave. If it's approved, and I'm sure it will be, I'll leave by train at 6:20 in the morning for Copenhagen. I'll get there at 8:30 that night.

After a couple days I'll take another train to Amsterdam. Or if I like Copenhagen I'll stay there the whole time. I'm not making real definite plans so it will be real flexible.

Yesterday, I made Spec. 4.

About me driving a car on leave. There's no doubt that I'll want to use a car. I'll probably be driving around within St. Louis a lot, out to Columbia, and possibly clear out to San Francisco. The army will give me a couple hundred dollars travel pay, which would allow me enough money to go from St. Louis to San Francisco. If I leased a car for a month, the travel pay would pretty well cover the expense. If it doesn't, I have enough money elsewhere to cover it. Money isn't much of a problem. The problem is I don't have access to information I need from a car rental company. About 5 minutes on the phone would clear up any questions I have. So, mom, could you, right now (it should only be about 11:45 or so, if I remember when the mail comes); look in the yellow pages under auto leasing and/or rentals; pick a good sounding company; call them up; and beset them with the following questions:

> Can a 19 yr. old drive a leased car (signed for by a person over 21) without a 21 or older person in the car __Yes x No
>
> Are any provisions made so that the car can be collected by the leasing company in a city different from which it was rented in? (specifically, from St. Louis to San Francisco ___Yes ___No
>
> How much would it cost to rent a car (a small one with good mileage) for 30 days? If this depends upon the mileage, how is the cost computed?

Mom, if the first one you try doesn't sound any good, please try another one. I would really appreciate it if you would do this real quick and send the reply back to me. I need the information to make my leave plans.

Oh. When will I ever come home on the legendary leave? (I realize I've been talking about it since October.) It all relies upon when and if they decide to send me to Viet Nam. The chances of my request for assignment in Nam being approved is about 100% -0%. I will almost definitely go. When is another matter. All I can say is it might be tomorrow, it might be a year from now, but all things point to April. The status of my order is this: The Dept. of the Army has acknowledged receipt of my form 1049. The Division Personnel Services Office (located on post, by the way, with all the other Division agencies and offices) has notified the company that I will be available for reassignment on April 5th. What determines this, I don't know. The Div. Personnel Services Office required a form on me to be filled out, signed by myself, and returned to them. The form stated where I would spend my leave, and what type of travel (air, boat, train, rocket ship) I would want from here to New York and to St. Louis.

So it seems like in April I will get my orders. Maybe.

Enclosed is a picture taken by a slick talking photographer who had me conned out of DM2.50 (.65¢) before I knew what happened. (thus doofless expression on my face) It happened right when I came out of the Mainz train station Feb. 6 for the carnival.

Scott

11 Mar 67

Clyde—

Read <u>Zorba the Greek.</u> I don't know if you'll be affected by it like I was, but I'd like to discuss it with you some time.

I'll be going to the 101st Airborne Division.

Probably be home on leave in April. I hope to get to San
Fran a week or so before I go so we can kick up. I'd hate
Like hell to go get my butt shot up without seeing you
first.

See you soon—probably.

Scott

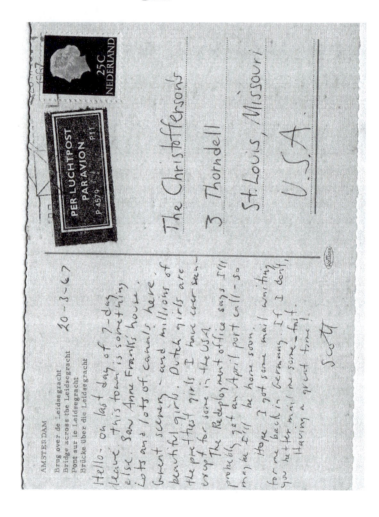

AMSTERDAM
Brug over de Leidsegracht
Bridge across the Leidsegracht
Pont sur le Leidsegracht
Brücke über die Leidsegracht

20-3-67

Hello - on last day of 7-day
leave this town is something
else. Saw Anne Frank's house.
lots and lots of canals here.
Great scenery - and millions of
beautiful girls. Dutch girls are
the prettiest girls I have ever seen
except for some in the USA.
The Redployment office says I'll
probably get an April port call - so
maybe I'll be home soon.
Hope I got some mail waiting
for me back in Germany. If I don't,
you better mail me some fast.
Having a great time!

Scott

The Christoffersons
3 Thorndell
St. Louis, Missouri
U.S.A.

24 April '67

These are my thots as I am about to leave for Viet Nam.

I see in Viet Nam fiery violence, lurking death, and U.S. B52's dropping countless bombs. The press has me thinking of Viet Nam as a hot, wet, bug-ridden hell hole where death and mutilation are the order of the day. I feel the same fear I used to feel when going into a fight with the biggest bully in town. But instead of fists of flesh and bone, I see all kinds of horrible, crude weapons trying to maul me.

No doubt a month from today I will be there. I am very close to actually having my fears realized and my curiosity fulfilled. I suppose that's the major reason I volunteered for duty there. My damn curiosity. Of course this type of motivation affords me with serious second thots. I want to see and do and feel as much as I can in my life, but a hell of a lot of good it'll do me if I'm dead at 20. This last thot bothers me quite a bit—whether or not the experience and possible fulfillment of my curiosity about war are worth the physical and mental risks involved. I am certain the risk is worth it—or else I wouldn't have volunteered. But once I get there—will the experience still warrant the risk? This I don't know and I won't know for a while. The answer to this question will be very important to me, because if it is to the negative, and I can't convince myself of one or more of the following, then I'll feel like an ass for risking my skin for nothing:

> The evil of communism (assuming it is evil—or why combat it?) must be stopped some-where.

> The cancer destroying Viet Nam (assuming the situation is malignant and is destroying Viet Nam) must be cured by the U.S. because Viet Nam cannot cure itself.

> Viet Nam is a calculated prelude to a larger con-flict. It is providing us with a foothold—

air bases, seaports, etc.—for a foreseen war with China.

All three of the above reasons are weak and it is clear I am unsure of the whole situation. Perhaps "4" is better:

The U.S., blundering along in its confused way, must be supported by its people even when it does apparent wrong, or else the good it can do will not be done. In other words, the injustice the U.S. may do here and there is tragic but unavoidable. Maybe these kinds of stupid things cannot be helped.

But perhaps the good-evil factor in all the above is not the key to the crisis. Then, what is? Well, survival has been the motivating factor among men for a long time. Probably since the beginning of man.

Maybe good and evil have little or no significance in man's struggles, whereas survival does.

In a death struggle, one of the contestants must die. Who's to say which one is evil or good? Does it matter? The good guy doesn't always win. Maybe survival is the thing that matters most, because unless you're alive, you erase the possibility of both good and evil. So, sure, good and evil are important—but life, good or evil, is more important. How so? Because good as well as evil live in a person; a man is neither all good nor all evil, he is capable of both. Here, I think, is his glory.

But how about the existence of good and evil after death? I don't know. But because of the possibility that <u>nothing</u> exists after death, I'm gonna try my <u>damnedest</u> to stay alive.

So I'm going to Viet Nam, perhaps to try to prolong the existence of a nation which is capable of good.

Because any nation (as any human life) is so capable, why in hell should I kill another one?

Maybe killing is the greatest evil of all....and I'm going there to perhaps do just that...why? ....because I'm in a dilemma about ....many things...but dilemma is life...my life, your life, everyone's life....thus blossoms the "Heads in your asses" theory.

So here we are, 3 billion or so of us, running around in circles, our heads up our asses, reproducing like mad, trampling under those who fall and have fallen, in an endless, senseless existence. But it isn't endless because someday the sun will fall down and kill every damn one of us; and it isn't senseless only inasmuch as life itself is senseless. And we are all burdened with or gifted with, or just possessed of life, and are all therefore owners of the dilemmas and senselessness of it.

The enormity of thrusting myself into the path of death has struck me. What am I doing? Life is full of danger, frustration, dilemmas, unanswerable questions, and ultimately, death. Perhaps in doing what I'm doing, whatever it is, whyever I'm doing it, I'm living. And that's all that counts.

But what of words like "purpose" and "direction"? Do these apply to life?

Man is a creature with a mind (which is probably his downfall) who wanders in his world, experiencing all the frustrations, agonies, joys and happiness and sorrow that is reserved only for man. To live man's life is to experience these things.

So, if, after all this gobbledygook of words, if someone asks me why I'm going to Viet Nam (let alone why I'm alive at all), all I can say is, "You don't fucking know, do you?"

I suppose, getting back to my thots on leaving, that saying goodbye to my parents and friends will be very hard...

Tell me if you think I'm on my way to being a total cynic.

Like an insolent, sensuous wisp of a girl
Luring me to delicious delights;
The prospect of travel and danger;
War draws me with Satanly might;
A wish to experience? A desire to die?
What in the world can it be?
That I, like a sheep am being led by a rope
To a certain deadly demise.

Chapter VII.
Vietnam

28 May 67

Hello everybody—
    Well. Here I am.
    As you know, I left Ft. Lewis the night of the
18th. We stopped en route at Anchorage and some airport
in Japan. We arrived in Cam Rhan Bay 19 hrs. after we
left Ft. Lewis.
    I spent about 20 hrs. at Cam Rhan Bay then flew
to Pahn Rang. That was Sunday. Monday we started "P
training," which is supposed to last 5 days. One company
of the 502nd (one of the 3 battalions in the brigade, the
others being 1/327 and the 2/327) got torn up pretty bad
so we were shipped to the front on Friday.
    We're near Duc Pho, which is pretty far north.
My first night here I slept on the ground without the
benefit of mosquito netting. The bugs bit me up real
good, so if I come down with malaria I won't be real surprised. But I have a cot now and some netting. We sleep
in tents. There is a 3 ft. wall of sand bags around every
tent. The terrain is hilly and green. The flat lands are
patched with rice paddies complete with authentic looking
conical-hatted workers in black or white pajama-like out-
fits. Choppers constantly are moving about. Phantoms,
too. Artillery rounds are heard all the time exploding
nearby. Altho the brigade has been here a month the immediate area is still unsecured—meaning Charley is about.
Apparently the infantry is running into a lot of North Viet
Nam soldiers. The enemy is well equipped. They wear
uniforms, are larger physically than the South Viets, are
well trained, they have the fastest firing machine gun in

113

the world (a Russian copy), their AK-48 is every bit as good as our M-16's (also a Russian copy), their mortars are effective, and they have Russian rockets. The only thing that saves us is our air power and artillery. Our tactic is to send out patrols, make contact, radio back for air strikes, reinforcements, and artillery. The kill ratio is 9-1. But big deal. There are millions of gooks and they can afford it. Another tactic is to send out Long Range Reconnaissance Patrols of about 6 men, not to make contact with the enemy, but to radio their location and then try to move out undetected.

Our military here is well trained and equipped with the best. MEDEVAC, the much-praised evacuation of wounded soldiers, provides great morale. The army here is capable of defeating nearly anybody. I can see and feel the frustration of such an army that is forced to settle for such darn limited objectives. Maybe we ought to blow up another Maine, or allow another Pearl Harbor. It seems that without an incident like that the U.S. is only half way about war, like in Viet Nam and Korea.

It is inevitable that we fight China anyway, so why in heck piddle away 160 or 170 men a week and billions of dollars in a half-fought war? We must either fight all the way or not at all. Why is the war "inevitable?" It is either fight them now or wait until they use the atomic bomb to intimidate some smaller nations. The loss of that smaller nation's economic and political life and our own industrial and human loss will be minimized if the war is fought before the Chinese get the bomb on an operational basis. Perhaps more important is the fact that Russia would like nothing better than to see the U.S. severely weakened, as we will be, in a major war against China. Then, with us so weakened, how could we do as we did against Cuba in 1962? The U.S. would lose its bargaining power as a result of an atomic war with China. Russia is right now supplying 80% of North Viet Nam's war goods. Isn't it awfully obvious what they're trying to do?

114

We should first admit the Chinese to the UN. Second, urge the British to leave Hong Kong and the Portuguese Macao. I urge this because most of the friction is political and racial anyway, East vs West and Mongol vs Caucasian. The removal of Western presence from Southeast Asia should be our ultimate goal. Third, we could leave Viet Nam now and pray that when China develops an operational arsenal of A-bombs, that she uses them against Russia. There is a good possibility of this because 1. Russia is more "West" than "Asian," 2. There are severe ideological differences between the two, and 3. there are strong boundary differences between the two. If this happened--that Russia and China went at it together-- it would be fine for us. China would be eliminated as a force to be reckoned with, and perhaps Russia would lose some of its bargaining power. At the same time as withdrawing, we could better our conditions with Russia, thus making China dislike them even more, and possibly entering into some sort of military pact with Russia and the other Southeast Asian countries. Also, in this first idea of withdrawing, it would be necessary not to allow China into the UN. For the whole thing to work, China must be frustrated there.

Another plan would be to allow China into the UN, therefore making possible UN action on her military aggressiveness. UN action would be tenuous so the U.S. must remain in S.E. Asia. To do so we could either nominally withdraw, or at least cease anything but defensive action, or we could carry on stupidly like we are, or we could sweep up to the Chinese border in the name of something or other holy, counting on that the Chinese will not cross the border in Force. If they did, we'll charge "foul" and fight them then. The political climate must be proper for the plan. The internal turmoil now in China would be ideal.

Whatever course of action we take, we must take it soon. Time can only hurt us.

Well, I'll get this in the mail now. I could run on forever but I know you want to hear from me.

I'm getting a great tan.

Scott.

P.S. I see I forgot to even tell you what I'm doing. I really lucked out and am operating the brigade switchboard. How about that? Will write more later.

1 June 67

Hi Kit!

Happy birthday.
We don't have a PX here so I couldn't get you a card.
I am outside of a town called Duc Pho. We have a beach where we go swimming. I'm getting a swell tan.
This makes 2 birthdays of yours in a row I have missed. I'll make sure I make the next one.
Well, I have to go on shift in a little while so I'll finish up.
Have a happy birthday.
These are called "piasters." They are the Vietnamese currency. 118 piasters make a dollar.
Love, Scott.

31 May 67

Hi John!

How the hell are you?

I am fine.

Actually, I'm hot and sweaty and am fighting off the damn mosquitoes (these mosquitoes are nearly as bad as Canadian ones, remember those?) and I am sunburnt all over. I have no swimming suit so I swam in the raw and have you ever had a sunburnt dick?

The fucking artillery is booming away 24 hours a day. Jets drop napalm and WP (white phosphorous) all the time. Helicopters are all over the sky. Machine guns make it hard to sleep and do you know that there are no girls around here?

Since the 101st came over here in '65 they have lost over 400 men. Medevac—the name for the helicopters that come in and evacuate the wounded—does a great business. Yesterday 3 men were killed and 6 wounded. Don't ever let anyone tell you this war isn't really a war. There's no other name for it, barring euphemisms.

I'm pissed off but if I was in the infantry I'd be even madder. As it is I have a relatively safe and easy job. I operate the brigade switchboard. I am close to the war physically and psychologically but the infantry is a whole lot closer. So I can see the war differently, or at least not so closely, as they can. This is good because if I had to do what they have to do I'd probably turn into an animal or go crazy. As it is I can observe and still be considered a participant. There's no one else except correspondents who can see it as I can. I have plenty of time off. A beach is 2 miles away. It's full of jelly fish and LARCs and men and supplies, but it's cool and refreshing anyhow.

The country is hilly and green. The valleys are low and flat and patched with rice paddies. The people are small and tanned and bowlegged. They wear hats that look like flattened cones and pajama like clothes.

Actually this is damn pretty country. Only the war makes it otherwise. I'll write you later. See you in a year.

Scott

3 June 67

Dear Mr. Carnachan—

It's been a long time between letters. I left Germany the 5th of April and got home in St. Louis that night. I stayed there for a month and went to Denver where I spent a weekend with the Jeromes and the Lavach's. Then I went to San Francisco and spent a week. The weekend before I reported to Ft. Lewis I stayed in Seattle with the Lautman's. I reported the 15th of May. The 18th I left— by way of airplane, with stops in Anchorage and Japan. I got to Cam Rahn Bay the morning of the 20th. The next day I flew to Phan Rang—the 101st Division's Replacement Depot. There I had 4 days of training, was issued weapon and gear, and was sent to the nebulous "front." I am now near Duc Pho, north of Da Nang.

Right now I'm in Signal Company but soon I'll be a combat writer with the Public Information Office. The two men in charge, a Major and Lieutenant, seem to be very professional and run a pretty good newspaper. They edit the brigade paper and submit stories to the AP and UPI as well as the Stars and Stripes and other news agencies. I got the job by accident—walking into the wrong tent looking for something else. They need writers (actually, reporters who go to the field and gather facts, who then write up a story which is edited) and I was interested. I wrote a couple of stories for them and they thot I showed enough ability to be accepted for the job. Now I am waiting for orders to transfer me from the Signal company to the P10. It shouldn't take more than a week. I think I'm going to like the job very much because I'll be able to see the war from a correspondent's point of view, a thing few soldiers can do. Not only that, but I'll get some good experience on reporting and writing.

At first I was surprised that Viet Nam is such a pretty country of rugged green hills, many streams and thatched-roof houses. Then I realized that war is the thing that makes countries so ugly. A pock marked hill here, a burnt out village there. It is not the country's fault, but the people's.

15 Jun 67

The letter was interrupted by my being transferred to P10. Yesterday and the day before were spent getting settled in and seeing how the office works. Day after tomorrow I go out to the field with a photographer. There are 3 infantry Battalions in the Brigade and P10 has a 2 man team for each battalion. We'll spend most of our time in the field—2 days out, one back in, then out again. I'm really looking forward to going out—should be a great experience. Yesterday I researched a story about a GI who spends his time off working with the Vietnamese. He goes out with borrowed supplies and performs a sick call. The Vietnamese situation will be improved by people like him, not by the infantry.

19 Jun 67

I'll make sure to mail this today or else it never will be. I got back from the field last nite. I helped cover 2 days worth of a sweep of the Song Ve Valley. There are approximately 10,000 civilians living there. The have cattle and rice and corn crops. The VC get a lot of supplies from them, so it was decided to sweep thru the entire valley, relocate the population elsewhere, and drive the cattle to the coast. The operation has been nicknamed "Chisholm Trail." I was with A company 2/327. We had no contact but rounded up several confirmed V.C. and a lot of suspects. About 600 civilians were helicoptered out while I was there. Tomorrow I'll go out again. It is a good experience—I get to see the country and the people.

It is a good experience, but a frustrating and sometimes painful one. To see people who are hungry and diseased and have to combat war as well, is not easy. You saw it and I am seeing it. There is only one thing I want to see for this country, and that is peace, so then the people can get back down to the business of living.

I am keeping a journal and in my next letter I'll enclose some excerpts. Maybe you'll find them interesting.

Scott

19 June 67

Hi Jim—

Hi! That letter you sent me was real cool until you got to the part about me being a switch board operator! Har-de-har! But don't worry—I got rid of that job and am now a combat writer. I work for a brigade newspaper and we contribute to UPI, AP, and other news agencies too. My job is to go out with the infantry and take pictures and find stories. Yesterday I got back from my first trip out. It was the first time I'd seen the war close up, and it wasn't nice. I'll tell you about it some time. Right now I'm too angry and kind of shocked.

But I like my job better than that stupid switchboard. It was driving me crazy. Operating a switchboard is no fun—not only that, but I got tired of people calling me a "titless WAC."

Jim- could you tell mom that there will be a check coming monthly made out to her and would she see to it that it gets put in a bank under my name? She might need my social security number—to start the account. Each check should be about $100 or more.

I'm also putting another $100 in "Soldier's Savings Deposit" so when I leave Viet Nam I should have about $2,500. I'm trying to get assigned to Ft. Carson

Colorado for my last 7 months. I should come back to the States for a leave after my tour here is over—that'll be in 10 months and 29 days. I'll get out of the Army in Jan. 1969. Next month I'll be halfway thru. Wow. Only 585 days till I get my discharge!

I know that you have nothing to do on these hot summer days and would like to do something. There is no PX out here in the boonies so I have no way of getting things I need. (But we get soap, tooth brushes, paste, etc.) Could you get to the store and buy me some stuff I need, put it in a box, wrap it up and mail it to me? There's $5.00 in it for you, plus a whole lot of thanks. Get the money from mom (tell her to take it out of one of the checks), and do it as quickly as possible. Have it sent airmail, it'll cost more that way but it'll get here in a week rather than the 2 months it takes by boat. Here's the list: 1 metal boy scout type mirror, 4 'bic' pens, blue ink, 10 or so spiral notebook, small ones about 6'x4' Make sure it's the one that you can fit in a shirt pocket.

You can probably get the above at Woolworths (and the mirror at Stix's Boy Scout counter).

The books, below, you'll be able to get at "The Book Nook" in Clayton for sure (across from the courthouse, the side opposite the bank), or maybe at Stix's book store. All paperback.

Catch -22

A Fine Madness

The Winter of Our Discontent - Steinbeck

 Sweet Thursday – Steinbeck.

If there is any room in the box left, put in those Kool-aid packages that are complete with sugar, the box shouldn't be real big. Mail it in the Stix Post Office – AIRMAIL. If you can't find any of the books, don't worry.

Well, it's now the morning of the 20th, and I have to go out to the field again. I'll stay for two or so days.

Scott

The enclosed was found in a V.C. bunker yesterday.

ARMYMEN BELONGING TO U.S. EXPEDITIONARY CORPS IN SOUTH VIETNAM

The Johnson Government has been dispatching more and more U.S. combat troops to South Vietnam hoping to turn the situation favourable to them. But the result is that: The more U.S. troops dispatched to South Vietnam, the greater their defeats will be.

The strategist attacking plan in the dry season in order to regain the initiative on the battlefield with the campaign « 5 Arrows » in the first months of 1966 completely failed.

Within 5 months (November 1965 – March 1966) the South Vietnamese people and Army ;

—Wiped out 114.000 enemy troops (including 43.000 U.S. and Satellites) 30 battalions — 141 companies (including 14 battalions and 22 companies of U.S. and Satellites).

— Shot down or damaged 1.440 air craft of all types.

— Destroyed 1.310 military cars (including 330 M.113 — M.118—M.14 amphibious ones) and 27 warships.

— On the central front of S.V.N. U.S. troops were attacked everywhere and received heavy losses. Here are the proofs about these losses in the recentitme.

— June 18 – 26-1966.

1.402 U.S. troops of the 101 Division of paratroopers and the First Air Mobile cavalry Division were killed or wounded by the L.A. at Tuy an (Phu yen province)

— July 14-1966.

The Gosoi post (Quaug-ngai province) 8 kilometres South of Chulai was attacked.

22 June 67

Hi Clyde—

How's it hanging? I assume you are in Palo Alto because if you were home you would have received letters to the family, and would have, once learning of my return address, immediately, with your usual lightning (**snap! crackle!**) fast speed, rushed a letter to me.

Having received no such letter, I take it you are in Calif. I am now giving you a chance to write me.

So how are things? What's the latest chapter in the "Lives and Loves of a grad-school Law Student?" And how's mom? All I heard about that was over the phone from Ft. Lewis when Jan said she was in the hospital. She didn't say what for. Jim, in a recent letter to me, mentioned that she was feeling better. What was she in the hospital for and how is she now? Please fill me in.

This fucking place is really something. We are up near Duc-Pho—we are now involved in Operation Malheur II, something probably in the news. Walter Cronkite should be having an 8 minute article on the 101st Division---"The Vagabond Division."

24 June 67

Don't know if you've heard, but I'm now a combat writer. I also take pictures. We put out a brigade newspaper and contribute to the UPI and AP and Stars and Stripes.

I go out to the field for 2 days or so at a time with the 2nd Battalion, 327 Infantry (Airborne). I've been out with them twice and tomorrow I go out again. Our last operation—nicknamed "The Old Chisolm Trail"—should have made the news back in the States. It was the biggest endeavor of its kind yet attempted in Viet Nam. Although it sounds like a mass kidnapping and cattle rustle, it is actually a resettlement program for 5,000 Vietnamese and 1100 cattle. They were in the Song Ve River Valley and were being constantly exploited by the VC. The purpose of the sweep was to evacuate the villages to a resettlement camp, and to drive the cattle down the river to the resettlement camp for distribution among the refugees. With no population to draw soldiers from, and no one to keep the crops, the Song Ve River Valley has been changed from a V.C. stronghold to a worthless valley. Months ago Marines probed the valley and met such stiff resistance that they withdrew. So did the 25th Div. However, the 101st met very light resistance, surprisingly enough. It was a well executed and effective operation.

Tomorrow a different operation begins. I'll be there to cover it with my trusty camera (Pentax Spotmatic) and pen. This job is ideal for me—I can jump from hotspot to hotspot like a correspondent. I can see the war close up without being forced to see it all the time, and I can step back and write about it. Not many GI's get to do this. I'm glad I've got the opportunity.

(With typical Christofferson finesse, I obtained this job by blundering into the wrong tent while looking for something entirely different. They said: no, this is not the place you're looking for. Me: then, what is it? Them: this is the Information Office. Me: Fine. By the way, what's it you do? Them: Oh, we put out a paper. Brigade paper. Me: Oh really: Do tell. They told me about it and I was interested. I met the officer in charge and he told me they were looking for writer-photographers. I expressed my interest, wrote some stories for him and—a star was born!)

So no longer do I operate a switchboard—I am now a daring photographer! a prolific writer! an amateur journalist! Hot damn.

I get to carry a rucksack, M-16 and ammo just like an infantry man. I have the privilege of being an American propagandist. Few men in the brigade even know of the existence of the paper. I'm afraid it's for the brass and the Army back in the States. This pisses me off. I think the paper is just for appearances. (What in the Army isn't? I'd like to know.) Notwithstanding, it can be a profitable experience for me. The officers in charge are pretty competent. Most of the guys I work with are OK. I think I'll get something out of it, experience wise and journalistic wise. Despite the fact that I must write "Army" type news and the probability that the paper isn't read by too many people outside of the office, I halfway like what I'm doing. A rarity for me in relationship to the Army.

Well. Enough about me and my job. Some about Viet Nam now.

From the ground or the air you can see the damage war has done to the country. Mud and grass houses have been shelled. Craters from artillery pock-mark the ground. Nearby rice paddies are deteriorating with lack of care. Bamboo and palm trees are being splintered—their torn ends are being dried and bleached by the sun. Streams are being re-routed by unnatural upheavals of the earth. Artificial ponds are created in holes left by 500 lb bombs.

Bewildered people in straw hats and pajama-like clothing are herded on helicopters to be sent to relocation centers. Their roots in the earth are severed as are their limbs above ground. Yesterday men of their own race came into their villages and terrorized them. They took their youth and their grain and corn and rice. They threatened old women and children. Today armed men in green clothing, bigger and whiter than they, came into their villages. They herded the people outside into a field—telling them to carry their belongings. Then they searched their homes, overturning furniture and ripping up floors.

Big helicopters came and carried the villagers away to "relocation camps." Medical aid and rice was given them (not enough, never enough), and then they were brought to a new place where they began to erect a new house and a new life. But there are only old men, old women, and children. A generation seems to have disappeared, either to the Army or to the VC or to death.

It will take many years to rebuild decimated families and start new ones.

I think war is probably the hardest on those who must live in it, not those who carry it on. There is a different kind of pain between being killed physically and seeing intangible things being torn apart. The latter pain, I suspect, is more intense and lasting than the first one.

There is nothing glamorous or even particularly dramatic about it. It is different than what the melodramatic TV reports make it seem. It doesn't even look the same as pictures show it. It contains things photos can't reveal; like the staccato rattle of machine guns, the whump of grenades, the concussions of the artillery, the whoosh of rockets, the roar of helicopters, the acid odor of people's sweat, the nearness of death and mutilation. The heat of a searing gun on your back, the stickiness of mud clinging to your boots, the hard-to-get-used-to feeling of being constantly wet. The lurking monster of futility which occasionally clutches your throat. The strangling loneliness that chokes you when you aren't busy. This and much more is apparent and real when you are actually here. It ain't nice, but it (the experience) reaches into part of your skull and shakes into consciousness cells of awareness which can be awakened in no other manner. To me, life should be spent awakening all those nasty little cells in your fucking head. And, man, I'm off to a flying start.

Write me a big long letter. Mail means a hell of a lot.

Scott

25 June 67

Hi John—

Guess what? I got a new job. It sounds impressive as hell—combat writer, photographer, but it ain't. I got it with typical Christofferson finesse, by walking into the wrong tent looking for something entirely different. They happened to be looking for more writers and photographers, so I applied for it and got it within 3 days. It really happened fast. What I do is go out with the infantry with a camera (a 35 mm Pentax Spotmatic) and a note pad. The outfit I cover is the 2nd Battalion, 327th Infantry, 101st Airborne Div., so if you see them in the news, you'll know that I was there. I've been out with them 3 times and I'll go again tomorrow.

It is ideal for me and I can actually see man at his

worst without having to endure it all the time—I come back at regular intervals to write my stories and turn the film in.

One thing bugs me, though. The crap I write has to be "Army type" news, which is news, all right, but only a certain kind of news. Only what looks good for the Army is printed. Like 3 days ago when someone fucked up and 12 million bucks of ammo blew up. We can't even have it in the paper. It never happened, I guess.

I guess the Cards are hot as hell, first place. Compared to Viet Nam, Germany was full of newspapers. I really have lost track—except for some sports and really big events, like Israel kicking shit out of the Arabs.

There is ice here, but the beer still is pretty warm. The ice doesn't last long in this heat.

Mail is slow—yours took 10 days. Also, note the change of address. I'm assigned to headquarters company now.

I sure hope Ray just waits to be drafted. I'd hate to see him waste an extra year or two of his life.

My sister is going back to college—in Denver in Sept. She's going to study nursing at Loretto Heights.

Clyde's working in California this summer.

Jim wrote me to tell me to have fun but be careful—one out of every 4 G.I.'s in Viet Nam gets V.D.! I guess he's growing up. Next year he'll be in 8ᵗʰ grade— the same year I first met Sue. Have you heard from her lately? Probably not.

In a letter from my mom I found out she had an operation. She also mentioned, in a funny story, that Carrie had come up to her one day asking her, "What's a prostitute?" I guess they're all growing up.

I had a swell time in Denver. My cousins and I kicked up pretty good. In San Francisco, Clyde and I had a ball. I stayed there a week. I put 800 miles on his TR-4 while he was in classes. Remember Buzzy Hamburg—a grade under us in H.S.? He was there. I also ran into

John Felder. When I saw Pat Deckert (Pam's older sister), she couldn't believe I had actually "volunteered" to kill people in Viet Nam. Instead of discussing it like I should have, I told her that we are all sinners and everybody's going to hell anyway. This really seemed to shake her up. I just wasn't in the mood to have a big conversation about it, tho.

My last nite in Frisco, Clyde and I blew $26 on a dinner in the most expensive place we could find. He is poor as hell and hadn't had a big nite out in a long while—but he promised to treat **me** when I come back. He's a real bright guy. It had been a year and 4 months since I'd seen him last and I never really realized what a great guy he was. He has come down to earth about a lot of things. Even had his heart broken by some fabulous girl. (He pointed her out one day and I damn near shit. He has damn good taste.) We talked a lot and had some great times. One night we went to a Law Banquet—I got pretty high during the 2 hour cocktail hour and wow was it funny. They had a real distinguished lawyer at each table—I made a great impression with him and all my brother's buddies.

I drove thru Haight-Ashbury and across the Golden Gate Bridge. The whole week was great.

In Seattle I had another good time. On the flight from San Francisco to Seattle I sat with a 20 year old girl who is going to Bible School in Frisco. She was going to Seattle to see her boyfriend who's stationed at Ft. Lewis. He's going to be a missionary and she's gonna marry him and be a missionary's wife and they both are planning to go to some under-developed country to save souls, once they get married. Talking to her was great, but it made me realize how fucking cynical I am. Whereas she could say, "I believe in Jesus," and be perfectly content, I can't and am in constant unrest.

Lately I've been going to Mass—it just goes to show that a war will make you do all kinds of crazy things.

128

In Seattle I had a ball. My cousins and I (I am
not related to them; their mother and mine were childhood friends) went swimming and hiking in the hills.
Marc, the oldest, graduating from H.S., and me and his
buddies went to a god-damn dance one night. It was
great. I such a young, good looking son-of-a-bitch! There
I was, on my way to Viet Nam, perhaps ("choke!") for last
few weeks of my life. The girls were great. I was dancing
with one particularly scrumptious young thing and we
were talking.

Me: "What high school do you go to?"

She: "I don't."

Hot damn, I thot! A live one! Trying to maintain
my cool, I said, "Well, then, what do you do if you don't
go to highschool?"

She: "Why, I go to junior high."

Good god, I thot! Christofferson, you are a lech-
erous son-of-a-bitch! Christ. The girls didn't look like
that when I was in J.H! They must be feeding them
Wheaties nowadays.

After the dance we went to the airport, snuck out
to the runways, laid down next to the runways in the
grass, and let a couple aircraft roar down (with their wings
directly over us as they passed) past us. Then we got up
and ran like hell, jumped over a fence, and sped away in a
car before the airport police could catch us. Wow. It was
crazy as hell.

Denny, a 17 year old sister of Marc, (good looking and smart gal) wrote me. I wrote her back, hoping
she'll keep up a correspondence. Never can tell what'll
happen.

Next time I'll write more about this place.

Scott

2 July 67

Hi Mom—

In case Jim didn't relay the message, (or if case he didn't get the letter), a check will come every month made out to you. I closed my bank account in Columbia while on leave and would appreciate it if you could open one for me. I don't care where it is. Each check should be for more than a hundred dollars.

Also coming to you will be a bond. I don't know if it will come every month or every three months, but it's a $18.75 bond. They finally coerced me into buying one.

I'm putting a hundred dollars every month into Soldier's Deposit at 10% interest. I'll have bou coup money when I leave here. (Bou coup, by the way, is Vietnamese-French-GI slang for 'a lot.')

This job I have is great. I have been out to the field a lot and have taken a whole bunch of pictures and written some pretty good stories. When the paper comes out, I'll send you a copy. This is pretty ugly and sad, the war. 'The Vietnamese people are pawns of great powers in a cruel game of international chess.' A Christofferson quote.

Denny Lautman sent me a can of brownies. Also a letter. Aunt Lordie sent me a silver St. Christopher medal—it is really a beautiful thing. But I don't wear it as this darn climate rusts anything. I don't remember if I mentioned it before but the Lautmans are a wonderful family.

I finally got your first letter, postmarked the 6th of last month. Got a letter from Jim—I hope he thinks being a 'Combat-photographer, writer' is a little more dramatic that a switchboard operator. Clyde hasn't written me yet—typical. Sounds like you're up and around pretty good. There's a chance I'll extend here. I should rotate back to the States in May (only ten months and days-wow!) and then spend until January there. But if I extend

I'll get out in November or October of '68. That's called an early out—means I have to extend here for 6 months. There's more money in it, too—there's a bill in the works to make $1800 for GIs who extend here for 6 months. It means I wouldn't come home until November '68, but it'll be worth it because 1. I'll get out several months early 2. If that bill passes I'll get bou coup money out of it, and 3. Stateside duty is awful—all spit and shine, and I'd rather be here than there, 4. the extra 6 months in this office would really help my journalism references, a photo and story book and the experience.

I'll definitely go back to the U. of M. , either to the Education School to be a history or English teacher or the J school.

John is working at Laclede as an accountant this summer. Roger Becker is still in Calif. going to the Army Language School. Ray Murphy is working again near Reno as a fire fighter. He is done with school I think- got a 1.0 this semester. He'll probably get drafted this summer. I don't know what Ted Myrick is doing this summer—which reminds me, please look up his address in the phone book so I can write him. He lives on an East Drive near Crystal Lake. An HE phone number I think.

A care package containing almost anything would be great. I asked Jim to send me one. Paperbacks run at a premium here. Toilet articles are supplied (free) by the Army, so I don't need anything like that. Pens, tablet, a nail clipper, metal mirror, books, etc. anything darn near. Old Time magazines. Envelopes.

I can't write anything for newspapers or magazines while I'm in the Army unless I clear it with higher headquarters. But I'm collecting a lot of background notes and some stories for future use. I might send some of this stuff home for safekeeping and for you to read.

I'm going out for a few days in a couple of hours. Today is Sunday (yes, we work on the Sabbath). Last night I had guard duty. This morning I went to Mass—

held under a thatched roof by a Chaplain dressed in camouflage garb. (There's nothing like a war to reconfirm one's faith. Even a hard core agnostic 'no-nothing' like me.) The weather is hot and the sky is clear. It rains in the afternoon now. Monsoon season is approaching.

Well, say hi to everybody for me. I'll write again soon.

p.s. Note that my address is no longer 501st Signal, but Head Quarters (H.Q.) Company!

Scott

26 July 67

Hello Clyde—

By way of celebration of the beginning of my third month I came down with malaria.

I had just returned from the field after 6 days when it hit me. Heat, then chills. I saw the medic right away. The next day I was sent to Chu Lai (just south of Duc Pho). I stayed there 3 days, much of it spend under ice to lower my temp. Then they sent me to Cam Rahn Bay where I now am. I'll be here for a couple of weeks.

My temp is normal now and I'm getting a lot of medication. It's almost good to have slack time, but I'd rather be doing my job.

I probably caught it while out in the field. That 6 days was longer than I normally spend out there, and that was due to the fact that it was an extended operation. I went out there (by helicopter, of course—I travel a lot by air, enough so I could qualify for the Air Medal by the end of the year) on a resupply mission as I normally do. The next day another resupply mission came and gave us rations for a total of seven days. Three days is the normal supply.

The next day we made a heliborne assault on a

hilltop near where two battalions of VC supposedly were. No contact. Although we found dozens of newly-dug bunkers and even boiling water and hot rice and corn in one place, we found no large number of VC. There were a few small firefights, tho, and several rucksacks found with women's clothing in them.

Most of the time we just humped, slang for walking, an obsession of the Infantry.

A comment on this war:

The US and Russia are waging another one of those "small" wars in which Russia refuses to get directly involved (although she supplies some 75% of the war goods sent to Hanoi), whereas the US does, and must.

In the July 14th (I think) TIME, it had a very astute article written on the Israeli conflict, and in it tied together the Israeli-Arab war along with the Vietnam war and a lot of other conflicts, like the Greek civil war. It also helped explain a lot of other incidents in post WWII that could have led to a war. The overall impression it left me with was that the Russians will commit themselves in every manner except physically—an important exception—that indicates that Russia is unwilling to face a nuclear war with the U.S.

It is obvious that had the Russians come to the aid of the Arabs, as they were almost bound to do (the Israelis had launched an attack on Russia's allies) it would have led to a major US-USSR war. By failing to do so, Russia lost much prestige.

In Vietnam, where the Russian non- physical presence is enormous (I myself have seen dozens of captured Russian-made weapons and anyone can realize how much Russian-made anti aircraft and surface to air missiles are present in N. Vietnam), the Russians stand a much greater chance of victory than in the Mideast, or anywhere else at the present. The reason is the nature of the war. It is a jungle war in which it is easy for a relatively small guerilla force to disrupt the government with relative ease for as long as they wish. And it's pretty depressing. The fighting men—I spend much time interviewing them—are extremely sick of the whole thing. Very few want to stay longer than their 365 days. With the exception of career soldiers and idiots (one guy I talked to has been here 35 months and he just extended again—he was a PFC--crazy as heck) the average "boonie-rat" counts his days and when he starts getting "short" he is the hardest person on earth to live with, especially if you yourself happen to be a "long-timer." It takes strong incentive to persuade this type of soldier to extend. The average line trooper wants only to survive his tour, board his Boeing 727 home, and forget this country even exists.

I think Russia, as well as China, will have to be negotiated with in order to end this war. Russia's commitment here has grown to an extent where, under the "right" circumstance, a nuclear confrontation between herself and the U.S. could come about.

Because of the growing costs of the U.S. commitment here, the U.S. should examine its whole foreign policy and be prepared to make some radical changes.

Some observations on the American fighting man (not including lifers who are not the traditional citizen force but the necessary core of the Army):

He is young. This is often reported and is correct. Many high school dropouts, young married men, frus-trated scholars, and youths out of high school who want to get their military duty out of the way, are found over here. Older men (like ages 23-27) are here, too, but in very small numbers. They were usually drafted after college and the number who did not become officers is small. Of course there are some military adventurers, but these fools are in the smallest number.

He is well equipped and well trained for this job, and, aside from going home, his biggest desire is to get a better weapon. The stories about the M-16 being a difficult weapon to keep operating are true. And so are the

134

stories that he would give anything for a Russian AK-47.
With the exception of the M-16 his complaints about
equipment are few.

I have read the statement that he is dedicated to
his job and the U.S.'s goals. I challenge this. The average
GI doesn't give a darn about this country, only half be-
lieves in the administration's goals here, and his only dedication is to come out of here alive. I have found that the
men in the rear who never have been in combat, are a lot
more philosophical and idealistic than those up front.
Naturally.

Few GIs respect the Vietnamese soldiers, people
or property. It is generally agreed upon that their army
isn't worth a fuck and neither are their women. I read in
the "Law" section of the July 14 TIME that there have
been some 12 convictions of GIs guilty of killing civilians
or prisoners in Vietnam. Don't dare tell anyone this or I'll
find myself in jail: but the average line-dog hates the
Vietnamese (or any Oriental); would rather shoot a prisoner than go to the trouble of guarding him until he can
be taken out; suspects civilians (and with good reason, too)
of collaboration with the Cong, so he'd like to shoot him
or her also, and in many cases, does. In general a trooper
considers anything bowlegged and slant-eyed fair game:
shoot first, ask questions later. Nearly all this is done for
survival—not out of bestiality. Any boy big enough to
carry a gun generally does. Women do, too. Any civilian
is likely to aid the Cong in one way or another. There is
some justification for killing them; mainly because they
are liable to kill you or see to it that Charley does. Those
GIs guilty of gross violations should be tried, naturally.
Some are merely blood thirsty. But, if every soldier guilty
of killing a prisoner or woman or child were tried, there'd
be lot of soldiers going to jail.

True, the soldiers kill so they themselves won't
die. But the damning thing about the whole thing is that
the average woman or child or peasant is helping the Cong

so <u>he</u> or his family won't die. The Vietnamese are, then, in the middle of a vise: with the Americans on one side and the VC on the other. The most tragic casualty of this whole fucking war is the Vietnamese people.

The object of the Americans is to, of course, kill the Cong and thus let the Vietnamese lead an unhindered life. The hard-core Cong is the object of the U.S. If he can be eliminated (and of course, if the NVA can be kept out of the country) then we've won. (I seriously doubt that (1) we can kill every Cong or stop their struggle, and (2) even if we do, many Vietnamese will be dead. And a lot of good that'll do. A free country with such a deci-mated population would swell—hell, we might as well let them be "Red than Dead.") So despite the above specula-tion, the U.S.'s goal is to kill Charley. Hard-core Charley.

Who is hard-core Charley? A lot of them are dead. Many of them probably are from North Viet Nam. Many are probably young S. Vietnamese men, as well as old survivors.

In examining their possible motives for fighting, I see great tragedy.

Many would like to desert and enjoy the soft, American-supported life. But they are aware that if they try, their superiors will kill them and/or their family. This poor guy is trapped on both sides. Many Cong have de-serted, and many more undoubtedly would but for fear for their own lives as well as their families.

Such a man is Ta`m (imaginary, of course). Like all VC 'cruits, he has been told in no uncertain terms that if he doesn't put out to his fullest, or if he tries to defect or quit, his family will face death. So he obeys orders and fights. He leads a miserable, disease-ridden life in the hills and many of his companions die in fights and from illness. He and two men share an old French Mauser and they have only 26 rounds of ammunition between them. A fun existence.

Then there is Nuygen. He is young and pissed

off. He saw his father executed by the VC. His village was strafed by an American jet, killing the rest of his family. He hates the Americans. He hates the Cong. On one hand, he could defect to the Americans, join the SVA and fight Charley. On the other hand, he could join the VC and fight the Americans. Either way, he's unhappy and full of hate.

Another Vietnamese man is convinced that the whites must be pushed out so his country can have peace. He was old enough to remember the French. The Americans are here now and there is still fighting. So he fights to push out the Americans. If there are only Asians on the continent, he reasons, then the Vietnamese, unhindered by any outsider, can resolve any differences and have peace.

I could go on and on with hypothetical characters (maybe I'll do a series of sketches some time, after I'm out of the Army, of course) but I won't. I'm just trying to show the entire tragedy.

There is the tragedy of the young American who loses a leg here and goes home crippled for life.

The bewildered peasants, exploited and threatened and killed from all sides.

The VC fighting to oust the Americans and unite his country.

Everybody involved is getting fucked.

The U.S. is getting tired of the war and wants to put an end to it. Johnson, the bastard, is continuing the war politically, compromising all the way until he will reach a point where he can't compromise any longer. Then the price of victory will be so high, and the cost of defeat so increased, that it won't make any difference which way he goes. It is obvious that he is trying to end the war as gracefully as he can, but unless he goes high hog one way or the other, he'll be forever doing it.

Perhaps he is biding his time till the elections, conscious that the public will not vote him out. Why he is doing this I don't know; he'll have to solve it between 68-

72 anyhow. The public couldn't stand his indecision for
another four years. Perhaps he wants a reaffirmation by
the people and some more time to deal with the war. In
any event, to me he looks like a fool for not deciding one
way or another. Maybe he thinks he has something up his
sleeve, though. I hope so, because if he is basing his policy
under the assumption that he will bring the North to its
knees, using this kind of pressure, then he's wrong as hell.

The Russians, of course, are delighted with the
whole mess. They would be happy for Johnson to lose his
shirt here, and even happier for a US-China war.

China is heavily involved here, as well as in other
SE Asian countries, and poses a terrible threat to all other
countries on this continent.

The biggest step, and the most productive one,
would be to admit China into the U.N.; get international
aid for her and the rest of SE Asia, and tell China that any
aggression will be met with all available measures, up to
and including the use of the bomb.

Create an effective treaty organization between
the Allies and the free SE countries. In short, carry out a
lot of the plans proposed by Johnson several years ago,
with the addition of letting China into the U.N.

If the rest of SE Asia is as poor as what I've seen
in Viet Nam, it really needs help. If SE Asia were reasona-
bly well off and had a strong government whose solitary
goal was to make its country as prosperous as possible,
then I think the troubles here would die down.

Of course, the crux of the whole thing is China,
and her latent aggressiveness. But I think if she is wel-
comed into the world and helped, and treated equally
(equally for international punishment as well), she could
fit in with the rest of Asia.

Realizing it's a big risk,and that there might be a
war with China anyhow, I think it's a lot more likely to
bring peace to Asia and would have more far –reaching
results, than our present course. The sequence of steps is

crucial. If we let China into the UN too soon, she will destroy it, making it a forum for her haranguing and harassment. We must first create an alliance between the smaller countries and ourselves, and begin aid.

Fuck it. My mind is getting too muddled for any more of this shit.

Now, for an exciting report on the continent-hopping, dashing and daring and debonair man of skin (aside from good looking); that champion of freedom everywhere: here he is, PROTOPLASM MAN himself.

Armed only with his steely determination! His tremendous intelligence! His super-toned body! His incredible good looks! (and his can of Mennen spray deodorant!) PROTOPLASM MAN relentlessly leaps from continent to continent in a never-ending search for his true identity, some common sense, and the plastic top for his Mennen spray deodorant!

After a harrowing childhood, during which he created an invisible, deodorant-proof shield about him to protect him from things too old for his young mind, our hero, PROTOPLASM MAN (Hooray!) cast aside the invisible, deodorant-proof shield and set out on his adventures.

A horrible monster made entirely of sticky ice water taffy was known to be lurking in far away Alaska. Our hero went in search of it. Encountering the gigantic ice-water taffy monster, PROTOPLASM MAN quaked with fear and respect. It was a frightening thing indeed, huge and icky gooey as it was. Not to defy legend, which clearly stated that it was no use trying to destroy the monster, PROTOPLASM MAN, zig-zagging as he ran, managed to evade the deadly quid. He ran and ran, too excited with fear and gladness to look back, but had he looked over his shoulder, PROTOPLASM MAN would have seen the ice-water-taffy monster smiling in a wise, pleased old Santa Claus way. Finally, when he was many miles away, the MAN OF SKIN stopped to regain his breath. He knew he was out of the ice-water-taffy monster's reach now, so he turned and looked, trying to detect the blob in the distance, but he had gone too far, and trees and houses and hills blocked his way. PROTOPLASM MAN, flushed with victory and joy, began to look over his costume to be sure none of the ice water taffy had stuck to him. A small piece had, on a remnant of his invisible shield just above his right heel. To find a piece of the invisible shield still partly covering him, PROTOPLASM MAN became slightly dejected. However, after eating his stolen ice-water-taffy, he felt much better and, flying home, nearly forgot about the lingering piece of invisible shield.

PROTOPLASM MAN returned home towards the end of summer time. Having faced the monster, and escaping with a piece of the taffy, the BI-PED WONDER (another name for our hero) was extremely proud of himself and nearly had forgotten the shame of finding the shield above his heel. Assuming his alter-ego of Scott Christofferson, PROTPLASM MAN posed as a college student. Learning of the evils and vices which inhabited campuses, our hero, fascinated and intrigued by them, came to know more about them. The more he knew about them, he reasoned, the better he could cope with them. (It becomes clear here that the MAN OF SKIN is not a super hero or super-villain, he neither perpetrates crime and evil, nor does he enforce the law and right.) After savoring college life, our BI-PED WONDER entered the army and became a paratrooper. He went to Germany where he indulged in much booze and boredom. Great Scarlet whores were many and easily had, and PROTO-PLASM MAN had many easily. Subsequently, he hurtled an ocean, a continent, and another ocean. Arriving in a beautiful land but teeming with bickering and quarreling, the MAN OF SKIN observed the countryside, and became depressed at the constant quarreling and bickering. The cause of the bickering was a gigantic, hideous monster,

covered with green scales and sprouting many sharp this-
tles all over its hide. It was a horrible sight to see, but
PROTOPLASM MAN was not too terrified to not maintain his cool. Casually, as he observed the monster, PRO-
TOPLASM MAN looked down at his right heel, above
which he detected no trace of the invisible shield.

So there you have it, readers, the never-before-
published TRUE account of PROTOPLAM MAN's life!
But the story does not end here, dear readers, no, it is just
now beginning, for our hero, that magnificent MAN OF
SKIN, does not know who he really is! He lost his true
identity in an accident suffered in his childhood, and his
never ending search is to regain that identity. But where
to look? How? It is a near-impossible task, and the average super-human would be defeated quickly—but not
PROTOPLASM MAN. Let's try to help him solve this
dilemma.

The only real starting point we have is his alter-
ego, Scott Christofferson. Who is he, anyway? He seems
to be a mild mannered youth, who by profession is a reli-
gious heretic, a neurotic, a consorter with whores, and a
masturbator. He has many firm beliefs, but some less firm
or more firm than others. Though he once sought truth
and good things, he now merely seeks; a mental vagabond, so to speak. Though he professes a disbelief in religion, doubts its value, hates Charlton Heston and scorns
the Stations of the Cross, he wears a cloth rosary with a
plastic crucifix around his neck. He thinks Mary Poppins
is the sexiest woman he has ever seen, and along with the
Good Witch of the North, is one of the two women he'd
most like to go to bed with. He suspects he is a little bit
crazy, and can't decide if he is a genius or an idiot. He is
positive he is unique, yet he fears he is Everyman.

This, be it as it may, is PROTOPLASM MAN'S
alter-ego. After seeing him, it's no small wonder our BI-
PED WONDER can't figure out who he is.

A few words on my immediate future. I want to

get the maximum early out I can get, 90 days, so I'll extend for 5 or 6 months in Viet Nam to get it. I hope to be a civilian near the end of October, '68, so, reeking with wealth and arriving in a state of hysteria on the West Coast, you can expect me to harass you for a while before I head for St. Louis. I hope to celebrate my 21st birthday as a civilian and in the States. (I'm going to take my R&R in March and probably go to Australia.) I'll work from Nov. 68 to Sept. 69. Should have enough $$ to live comfortably and perhaps loaf a little in the summers. I might go to business school. Or Journalism school, and eventually start a magazine. Or Education, but I doubt that. But I'll worry about it when the time comes. In any event, I'm going to go to college.

This letter got a lot longer than I intended; it's been the first time in a while I've been able to sit down and really write.

Realizing your post haste double time in responding to letters, I won't give you my hospital address.

I hope Jan makes it at Loretto, if she doesn't it will be a killing blow to her.

I agree with your "selective listening" theory. I catch myself doing it all the time, and I can remember in the past when I have done it.

I enclose an outrageously funny letter Kit (her camp name being Rusty) sent to Mom. I think she will be one of the better adjusted kids.

Apparently Dad got an award for his part in the development of the CAS[6]. Did you see the article in the 21 July TIME? Didn't mention any names or anything, but sure built up the project.

I await with bated breath for news on your love life, your job, and your half hour as a hippie.

Scott

P.S. If you detected any excessive self criticism in my self

---

[6] *collision avoidance system, a program for reducing midair collisions*

analysis, chalk it up to the rather depressing effect of having malaria.

6 Aug. 67

Hello everyone—

How's everything? Right now I'm sitting in an air-conditioned library. Later on I'll go to the beach and stop for a soda afterwards, and tonight go to a movie. Last nite there was a Filipino band and 3 beautiful dark skinned go-go dancers. Needless to say, they caused pandemonium.

Does it sound unreal?

Sure feels like it is. After spending most of the last month and a half in the boonies (that 2 days out, 1 day in is turning out to be wishful thinking) the luxuries of this place are really intoxicating. Electric fans, ice in quantity, French fries and burgers, and—get this—beds with mattresses and SHEETS! Three months ago I took all those things, and more, for granted.

Decent books, too. Cooper's Creek, a good one about the out-back of Australia; Laurence of Arabia, an impressive biography of an intriguing figure; some book by an Australian about writing short stories – Be Your Own Editor; and a book I'm now reading, The Life of Buddha, by some French scholar.

The movies here aren't so hot. The Army seems to have a knack of procuring mostly rejects. Once in awhile they get a good one, but rarely.

And there's a TV station here too. Except for sports, the medium needs help. Want to know what show is most popular and rates the biggest positive reaction out of the men? "Combat." "Batman" is scorned by most everyone, and for good reason. The show is absolutely rotten.

Except for feeling weak I'm pretty much recovered. For 10 days I took medication 3 times a day and was pretty much restricted to the ward. But now I have relative freedom and am feeling pretty good.

I don't know why Johnson is bothering to send 45,000 more men if he plans to fight the same type of war. Please send me the "Letters to the Editor" address of the Post Dispatch. It should appear somewhere in the Editorial page.

My mail is being forwarded to me but I haven't gotten any yet. So I can't acknowledge the dozens of letters I know you all have sent me in the last few weeks.

Only 447 days left.

Scott

8 Aug 67

Clyde,

I had a good idea just now, as I'm sitting in the library at Cam Rahn.

If you want some actual photographs, unexpurgated of the war as it really is, let me know. Since I can't get film here (the office keeps close track and theft is next to impossible), you could send me 35mm film in the mail. I could send back the exposed rolls and you could get them developed.

Of course, as I'd like to have some record of this place, I'd be willing to pay for it.

I understand they x-ray the mails so appropriate markings on packages would be necessary. Let me know what you think.

Did you get my last goliath letter? In my fever and muddle-mindedness I cant remember if I addressed the fucking envelope!

Scott

8 Aug 67

Hi Jan—

Thanks for your letter.

Sounds like your job was pretty interesting. Kit

sent mom a funny letter which Mom sent me which I sent to Clyde. She wrote it while at camp and it was a real terrific letter. When I was in Denver they were all looking forward to seeing you, so I know you must have had a ball—those people sure know how to give you a good time. Too bad you missed Toni Jerome, tho, she's a real cool girl. I heard Jerry was in the Army so I wrote him, haven't had a reply yet tho. Tell me what courses you're taking. And I know what you mean about chemistry—Mr. Bassman gave me a "d" or two when I had it. I never was any good at it, either, so don't feel like the lone Ranger.

You asked me when I got here and when I'll be home: I got here May 20 after leaving May 18. What happened to May 19 I haven't been able to figure out yet. I think I'll extend here for about 5 months past my 12 month tour in order to get an early discharge. Normally I wouldn't get out of the Army til Jan 24 1969. However, by extending for about 5 months I'll get out in late October '68. And I'll have that much more $ too. So that's probably when I'll be home—Oct. 68. Only about 442 days.

I guess you heard I'm in the hospital recovering from Malaria. My job's OK. I've had a photo published as well as 5 stories. Two of the stories were published in the Army Reporter as well as the Brigade paper. And another story will be published in the Brigade annual magazine—"The Red Garter Platoon" is the name of the story. It was the best one I've written so far. About a platoon of infantry who wear red garters around their heads. The Platoon Leader, a lieutenant, had found a red garter in a VC hospital they cleared out in Song Mao. He put it around his head. Soon everyone in the platoon wanted one, so the Lt. wrote his fiancé at Michigan State for help. She and some coeds got together and sent letters and red garters (which they wore a day themselves) to the men in the platoon. Soon everyone had one, and as many leave for one reason or another, the coeds still send them. It's become kind of traditional.

The stories I write are purely propagandistic. Only "nice news," or junk that looks good for the Army. No stories about death or destruction. I couldn't write in the story that "The Red Garter Platoon" has another nickname, only far more grisly than publication would allow. I don't write about Americans dying—only VC. It makes me angry—the hypocrisy and prostitution I let myself indulge in. But that's the way it goes.

Actually I'm a lot more satisfied and less angry than the above makes out. Sometimes I just get depressed about this stinking place.

I wish you loads of luck at Loretto and BE SURE to write and let me know what's happening.

Write ya soon—

Scott

16 Aug 67

Hi, all—

Just a quick note to let you know what's up. I'm still at the hospital and will be for a few more days.

Only one letter has been forwarded to me, from Roger Becker, so I haven't been able to acknowledge what I'm sure are scores of letters from you.

Like I said in my last letter, I've been spending my time on the beach (getting back that tan the jungle's darkness took away), reading, going to the flicks, and just lazing around. For a while I was pretty weak and tired but I'm getting better and feel about normal now. Just for the record, the kind of malaria I had was viceferous (sp?). Supposedly the worst you can get.

Will write when I get back to my unit. They are, by the way, operating close to Chu Lai now.

Scott

HELLO CIVILIZATION!
22 Aug 67
Chu Lai

Hi all!

I'm back up front. We're operating near Chu Lai and have had some fairly heavy contact.

Several letters were waiting for me when I got back. Two from Carrie and one from Carl. I know there are dozens more somewhere, because I didn't get any in the hospital, so I assume they are floating around somewhere.

Carl asked me if the prisoners released by some paratroopers were in our area. They were. Elements of one of our battalions walked right onto it and found some twenty-odd prisoners. Of course we made it up to be something really fantastic (which it wasn't) and our office had a field day of it. NBC and everyone else was up here begging for details. It made swell propaganda.

I doubt if I'll extend. I want out of this sorry place as fast as possible. Like, in 270 days.

I thot of a way for the U.S. to gracefully extract itself from this mess: see to it that anyone but Ky[8] and his partner win the elections. Almost all the other candidates want to cease fire and negotiate. It's either that or something similar or carry on as we are now until we get into it with China.

Jerry Lavach wrote me back. I was glad he was drafted and didn't enlist. He hates it, which is about as typical a reaction as you can get.

Like a lot of other people, I'm pretty well dissatisfied with Johnson's administration. A pretty crude joke making the rounds here is the question: Where is Oswald now that we need him? Of course I don't feel that way,

---

[8] *Nguyen Cao Ky, Prime Minister of the Republic of Vietnam, 1965-67*

but I'll probably vote for someone else in '68, even if the best the GOP can do is Romney and Reagan (if they run on a peace platform).

Enclosed is a copy of this week's paper. It has been changed from "The Diplomat Warrior" to the "Screaming Eagle." Different title, same propaganda. I haven't any stuff in it because I've been gone for a month. I'll keep on sending them, tho.

Think of me and all the other GIs tromping around the jungles here, and pray for peace.

I'll write again soon.

Your hero and mine,
Scott

Sept. 12 '67

Hi everybody!

Got your letters of Sept. 1 days ago, but we went out on an operation the next morning. The enclosed paper was printed way ahead of time and doesn't have a story of mine in it. Next week's should, tho.

After I got out of the hospital Aug. 22 I went out with the infantry, which was operating near Chu Lai. Then we came in and moved back to Duc Pho, for several days' rest and a 7 day operation. A couple of days ago we moved back to Chu Lai again and rumor has it that we'll be here till Christmas. Bob Hope never performed for the 101st because it's been in the field when he comes, but it's hoped we'll be in so we can see him.

It was good (and weird) to hear your familiar voices so far away. Mom, pay for the call out of my account. I don't have a lot more to say (for a change!) so I'll sign off now and write again when I do.

Scott

21 Sept. '67

Hi Clyde—
I finally got your letter written July 19. Nothing like speedy service, what?

Your job at Philco sounded interesting. So did your half hour as a hippie.

But what really sounded neat was the bit about the girl! I'll be glad when I get back into it.

We moved from Duc Pho up to Chu Lai. The only thing really different about it is that Chu Lai has a strip, which is by the way, a welcome thing for yours truly as my hands were sprouting red hairs and I was going insane. But now that we've been here a while the hairs are returning to their usual green tint and my mind is functioning at its usual neurotic rate.

A little about my job:
I've been staying for 6 and 7 day stints. I have been doing such a good job covering my battalion that they took the other guy off it and put him with another battalion.

I've been writing a lot of hokey shit, but they eat it up. Stars and Stripes has carried some of my stories—which is as far as our junk goes—so I've gained some prestige around the office.

I'll probably extend for a safe job in the rear. I figure that an extra 5 months will be worth the extra $, the early discharge, and will be just as safe and easy as stateside duty. So you won't see me till Oct. '68.

NBC is here. The will begin filming an hour-long documentary of a Negro platoon sgt. The platoon happens to be in my battalion and I know everyone in it. Wow! I'll get to see people I know on T.V.!

Frank McGee will be here for the filming. They are working thru our office, so we know everything going on.

Hot Damn! Once more the war will now be

brought into the living room—free and sterilized by 10,000 miles of flight from the stink and horror of it all.

It's becoming apparent to me that I'll either become a great cynic or a great philosopher. Which, I can't tell.

I got a letter from Jan a few weeks ago. She seemed depressed and discouraged.

Thanks for the film—but next time send Kodak Plus-z pan film, PX 135-36. The color film you sent was good—too good, in fact, for an amateur like me. Not only that, but the light sensitivity of it and heat sensitivity of it is hard for use in this climate. The film I suggested is black and white.

Wait one...think-think...now that we're near Chu Lai, and therefore near PX's, perhaps I should buy the film here and save a lot of trouble....consider, consider....Yes, that sounds good...formulate, formulate.....I will buy the film here and send it undeveloped to you. How's that sound?

A pal of mine died the other day and here is how I found out. I was out at a Tactical Command Post, from which the companies coordinate about. It's located in the boonies usually atop a burnt-off hill. 105 mm howitzers and mortars as well as a platoon of infantry protect it. Sand bagged positions dot the hill and tents house the brass.

"Hi man, what's happening?"

"Oh, not much....A LRRP[7] got killed day before yesterday."

"Yeah, I heard. Know his name?"

"It's a common enough name. Let me think."

"I heard one got killed, but I didn't get the name. I know some of the LRRP's."

"Real common name."

"An RTO?" (radio operator)

---

[7]*Long Range Reconnaissance Patrolman*

"Yeah, I think he was."
"Wasn't Hines, was it?"
"Yeah, that's it, Hines."
"Oh."
"Know him?"
"Yeah, I knew him."

A poem I wrote:

When I leave this tortured land,
In Some more peaceful place I'll stand,
I'll raise my arms and lift my voice,
"Know something funny?
I had no choice."

I'll write again soon.

Scott

21 Sept. '67

Dear Jan—
Howdy!
Mom said you were reading East of Eden and that you like it. I read it in Germany and it really bowled me over. What a book! Did you get the Biblical references? (Adam, the title, etc) Tell me what you think of it. Since I've read it, we can carry on a real intellectual sounding dialogue about it. HAR-DE-HAR!
A couple of my stories made Stars and Stripes. It means something because that's about as high as our junk reaches. Hot-damn.
I'll probably extend over here for a nice-safe rear job. That means you won't see me till Oct. '68. But just think! I'll be almost 21, be a civilian, and have a brand new car! We'll be the coolest brother-sister team going. Gosh!
Keep your eye on the Sports section of the Post-

151

Dispatch for a group picture of a bunch of 101st hard-core paratroopers and a Vietnamese kid wearing a Cardinal T-shirt. I'll be in it. Wow!

Jan, you mentioned in your last letter about being embarrassed. Don't be. It isn't anything to be embarrassed about—especially between brothers and sisters. Just don't get stuck in a rut—that would be embarrassing. I'd have to fly home to unstuck you, and be AWOL.

Somewhere at home there are a bunch of books of mine—probably in the bach-pad. One you oughta read is Burning Bright—(another one by Steinbeck). It's real short, easy to read, and written in a revolutionary style that combines the play and the short novel. The story is gripping and really hit me. Also try Pastures of Heaven if you like Steinbeck. It's a bunch of life stories of some inhabitants of a valley in S. California. I really enjoyed it. As a matter of fact, I dig anything by Steinbeck.

As far as this lousy war goes—I'm against it. The U.S. should not force its culture on anybody else, and that's about all we're doing here. We ought to leave Asia to the Asians, Europe to the Europeans, South America to the South Americans, Africa to the Africans, go home and worry about our society. Why mess with others when we can't even handle our own? If we aren't careful we'll over extend ourselves just like Rome, Spain, France, Portugal and Britain did. I don't think we are capable of doing all that we must do to continue our policy of meddling with the rest of the world. Now is the time to return our sphere of influence to the Continental United States and learn to live among ourselves.

So if you elect me president...

I gotta go now.

Keep writing!

Scott

Have you heard the cynical joke, very popular over here: "Where is Lee Harvey Oswald now that we need him?"

21 Sept. 67

Hi John—

Right now I'm kinda in a foul mood but I haven't written in a while so I'll write anyway.

Don't come in the Army. Go Navy or Air Force. Don't go in the Marines. Stay out in the water or up in the Air but don't be on the ground. I've seen it all and it is really lousy.

I've been shot at, I've carried dead men, and now, several days ago, I had a buddy killed. Fuck it! I've been scared to death, wished I were, had nightmares about me mowing down thousands of Gooks with an endlessly firing machine-gun, and found myself heatedly tracking down VC with the rest, just like dogs after a fox. I've seen courage, cowardice and insanity. Brutality, cruelty and slaughter. I've seen it all and I wish I hadn't.

Results: I believe man is a suicidal, masochistic, egotistical nut. I have found in myself all those things and more.

I want to see this fucking war ended before more guys die in vain and out of political blunder.

War is the ultimate evil and I want to see man save himself before he discovers the ultimate war. That wild hair hasn't been shorn. It's become malignant and I've matured from an angry boy to an angry young man. I hope I live to mature further. I suspect the next phase of maturity will be either that of a total cynic (which is the easier of the two) or a wise, calm philosopher. A third alternative, actually a regression, would be insanity.

Believe it or not, I like life too much to go crazy. I admire man's good traits too much to become cynical, so I guess I'm doomed to become the sagacious philosopher.

My sister had another, more mild, crackup. She won't be going back to school for a while longer (if ever). Apparently she's optimistic and enthusiastic about adjusting to life, and with her determination and guts I have no

153

doubt she'll make it. I am anxious as hell to get home and see her as well as the rest of my family.

Myrick wrote me. Unlike most of my buddies, he hasn't progressed much since h.s. graduation.

I read about Jim Janney climbing Mt. McKinley and nearly getting killed.

Do you know Wayne Scaturo? He went to Ladue for awhile, moved in his senior year. He's an infanty man in the brigade. Graduated '66.

Jim's starting 8th grade. That's the year I met Sue in. I can't believe he's that old now.

Carrie's in 6th. She's one of those smart, cute little girls that's doomed for class presidency or something.

Kit's in 5th. She's going to be an impish, good looking girl who'll attract guys by the hordes.

Carl is in 3rd. Frank is 2nd. They're too young to comment on, except I imagine they're destined for typical Christofferson good looks and genius.

Well, I'm not as pissed off as I was when I started the letter. Maybe it's good therapy.

I'll probably extend for a nice safe job in the rear. So chances are I won't be home until October '68, but when I get back, I'll be a civilian, and loaded.

I'll write again soon.

Scott

20 Sept 67

Hi all—

I've been busy spending much time in the field. Two stories of mine got published in the Stars and Stripes. Couple others made Army Reporter. Just got in after 6 days a couple hours ago. Good to have all that mail waiting.

Some guys from NBC are here. Frank McGee will be here too. Something about an hour long documentary on a colored platoon or squad sgt.

I hope Jerry doesn't have to come here, but if he does, maybe we can get together.

Been thinking a lot about whether or not to extend, and have decided that if I can get a nice safe job in the rear, I will. Then I'll be out in Oct. 68 – about 10 days before my 21st birthday.

I get to see a Post Dispatch about once a week—saw a story on a guy I went to high school with climbing Mt. McKinley.

Expect to see a picture of some guys of the 101st and a Vietnamese boy with a Cardinal t-shirt appear in the Post-Dispatch. I'll be in it too.

I met a guy who graduated from Ladue a year after myself. I didn't know him then, but we had a good time talking about people we knew. It's funny how everything changes so fast after H.S.

It was good to read the G.I. bill increase was approved. I'll get $130 a month when I go back. Been thinking a lot about that too, and will probably go to a JC in St. Louis for a couple semesters before I go to a big college.

Just to give you an idea of the kind of stuff I write—as nothing has been in the Screaming Eagle yet—when I got back this morning I wrote up two stories: 1 on a guy who in a recent firefight, had a bullet hit his chest and fall off (it was fired from a great distance and ran out of steam); tripped a booby trap which failed to go off; walked all over a mine field and escaped unscathed; and finally, to top it off, found a gaping bullet hole in the radio on his back once the fight was over. The other story I wrote was about a recon platoon (the "Hawks") and a raid it made on a VC village.

Two other stories, which I'll do tomorrow, 1. about a guy who's been getting a lot of mail from his home town-San Diego, and 2. about a Sgt. who stood on a mine for a half-hour--afraid to move--until engineers came. Then, while the company commander stood ready to drop sandbags on the "bouncing Betty" mine, the Sgt. dove for safety. The Capt. dropped the sandbags on the mine (which is supposed to bounce waist high before exploding—this inflicting more and worse casualties) and then he too dove for cover. The mine was a dud, but it'll make a great story.

21 Sept. '67

Today I have a day of relative slack-time. I was supposed to go back to the field but won't until tomorrow. We will take the pictures of the St. Louis people today for the P.D.

Well, I better go now.

Keep the letters coming—send me the address of the Editor of the Post Dispatch.

I have found that articles not concerning military matters don't have to be scrutinized by my superiors. So I'll start collecting rejection slips soon.

Yes—I am proud about my sainted name appearing in the vestibule.

Scott

5 Oct 67

Hi Clyde!

Happy birthday! How's it feel to be so fucking OLD?!

How's the life of a professional student?

About your last letter: (1) Did you lose your scholarship? (2) will your graduation from law school be delayed thru you carrying only 11 hours? (3) did you know $1 will buy me 5 joints here? I was surprised to hear your story, and now I've decided to experiment a little with it myself. I'll let you know how it turns out.

About assorted things: (1) could you get some film mailers and send them to me? Perhaps from a photo lab. I could mail the film directly to them, and address the stuff to you, who in turn could order copies for yourself of any ones or all if you want, and then send prints to me. Keep the negs in a safe place. I'd just lose them here. I've got a lot of exposed film ready to go. As it turned out, the labs here don't do a good job. (2) I'm going to start investing in a good complete camera outfit. I'll start with a Pentax Spotmatic, wide-angle lens, and a telescopic lens. (3) Enclosed is the wrinkled, uncorrected and generally sloppy typewritten copy of several fairly recent days of my journal. (4) When I extend I'll go to Special Forces, with about the same job I have now. I hope. So when you see me next Oct. I'll have a Green beanie on. Hot-dog. (5) My faith in Vietnamese whores has been redeemed. There are some good ones.

A general comment on the evolution of "the Kid" (myself, of course):

I really surprised myself by trying to kill a man, in two incidents, the last time out. The first one was in an ambush. We were out on patrol to try to recover some equipment we left behind the night before, when we fled the hill we were on due to VC mortar fire. All the equipment was gone. But then we saw some armed VC coming down the trail. We set up a hastily organized squad-sized ambush near the trail. I had no camera at the time so I couldn't take pictures. My adrenalin was up and I really was eager for the VC to walk into my sights. I don't know, maybe the animal instinct for blood is in all of us. For most people, it finds an outlet in some harmless way. In a situation where killing a man is acceptable, (God: any institution where such a thing is the primary goal, is evil!) the instinct is manifested in blood and death. The VC walked into us and I sighted on one and pulled the trigger. In my excitement I had forgotten to chamber a round. So nothing happened. There was a brief, fierce flurry of automatic and machine-gun fire and it was over. I hadn't fired a round. As I analyze the emotion I had felt

prior to the first shot, I can compare it to the emotion I
feel that comes after I have negotiated prices with a prosty
and am following her to the back room: Intense sensual
awareness, tenseness, shakiness that is caused by adrenalin,
a desire for quick and climatic action. Just like walking up
to the plate, behind two runs in late innings, a man on
first and thirds, two outs and a solid single or double will
tie the game. Or the feeling just before the lineman drops
the puck in the first face-off of a hockey game. It's weird.
It really is.

The second incident is described in the typewritten pages.

The more experience I have over here, the more I
detest it all.

I'm crude as hell, excitable as hell, oversexed as
hell, will do any crazy god-damn thing for kicks, and am
probably crazy as hell. God is a myth; but I wish I were
weak enough or strong enough or had whatever it takes to
believe in him. But I can't.

Paradoxically enough, the whole thing is pretty
interesting. Someday I'll write a book or novelette on how
this place affected me. The psychology of the whole horrible mess is somehow fascinating.

Now, tell me war doesn't do some strange and
awful things to people.

And tell me how I can say that man is really
something pretty cool? And he fascinates me? And his
reactions to all sorts of disgusting situations really interest
me?

I think I might have the temperament to make
some kind of a writer (or lunatic).

As I've been writing this letter, I've been letting
my thots wander and now I'm thinking about what I'll do
when I get out. I think I'll get some kind of a degree in
college, mostly because the life of a student appeals to me.
Then travel a few years in Europe, the mid-east and other
places. Then come back, get a VA loan, and buy or start a

small business, write on the side, and live to about 90.

Well, have a good birthday, kick up, and write. Also, don't forget the film mailers.

Scott

(I'll write again soon. It seems to be good therapy.)

5 Oct 67

Hi all—

Everything's fine here. How are things there?

In case you're wondering why I haven't sent you a copy of the "Screaming Eagle," it's because we ran out of money and haven't had any editions since Sept. 13. However, we have recently been financially reinstated so Oct. 16 we'll be in print again. Wow.

And in case you're wondering why I haven't written, it's because I've been busy and haven't had a lot of slack time.

I'm thinking about extending again. I've seen one side of the war and I'm anxious to see the other. So if I extend, it'll probably be for the Special Forces PIO, in Nha Trang.

If I extend, it'll only be for 5 months extra. To get a leave I have to extend for 6 months—but leave time is still Army time, so I'll just extend for 5 months, get the maximum early out (90 days) and be a civilian in Oct. 68.

I've been here for 140 days; I have 226 days till a year in country; and 389 days until I get discharged.

Wasn't so long ago that I remember having over a thousand days to go.

Mom—in your next letter please tell me how much I have in that account. Did you get the card with my signature on it?

I read how LBJ signed a 7 mill. bill for flight safety: any relation to McDonnell's thing?

Write and tell me vas es los.

Scott

159

September 1967 Essay

Towards afternoon, dark clouds swell up to the west and ominously expand their aerial domain until they hover above you.

You can see sheets of rain in the hills westward, and gradually the rain moves toward you. Men drop what they're doing and crawl into their poncho-constructed hooches. Simple canvas tents, staked down on four corners with a tall stick in the center.

The shower is over in a few wet moments. But the impending deluge hastens the men to utilize the break to ready themselves and their equipment for the night.

Sunrise and sunset are the most beautiful times of day in this country. The dampness of the night's rain sharpens the color of the landscape and as the sun creeps above the hills to the east, the countryside appears beautiful almost to being a prop.

Misty clouds hover in the valleys and between hills. As the orange fireball rises, the grey shroud of night and clouds vanishes.

A single crack shatters the dawn. Men scurry behind rocks. We are in the open and hills around us invite snipers. Two more shots split the day. One round ricochets off a rock very near me, leaving a dusty white scar in the boulder. The artillery officer calls in artillery fire on likely locations of the sniper, for we can't see him or tell where he is. The 105's boom in smoky rounds. Adjustments are made. The distant pop of the guns, the round cutting through the air above with a light whistle, the visible burst and destruction, then the boom as the impact reaches our ears.

A day later.

We jumped off the chopper as it hovered 6 feet off the ground. As we jumped into the high grass the chopper's 60 cals rattled away, providing covering fire. Wave after wave of the birds came in, hovering momen-

tarily as their cargo jumped off. No enemy. We organized
and moved out. Several platoons went north. We went
south and set up for the afternoon and night on a thickly
wooded knoll.

It rained like hell—I suppose the monsoons are
upon us.

The next morning we "saddled up" early and began what turned out to be a 4 hour march through very
thick vegetation along a creek bed. The creek led down
into a small valley, and as we broke out of the jungle we
came to tended rice paddies. We followed a trail and
came upon fresh tracks.

Further on we spotted some grass hooches. We
cautiously entered the small village. Women, children,
animals, and a man. We made him squat down and the
interpreter, further back in the column, was called up.

A search of the village began. Suddenly a GI
shouted, "Get him! There he is!"

My adrenalin shot up. Everyone turned and
looked. I saw him, no more than 30 feet away. I raised
and fired my weapon, but he ran behind a bush. Everyone
was shooting; a lot of them didn't even see him. Then he
came out into the trail again—running. I wasn't concerned that I might be killing a father or a son or a husband or a lover; I automatically and with full animal in-
tent to kill raised my 16 to fire. It misfired. Bad round.
Damn. I pulled back the bolt to empty the chamber and
put another round in. But it was too late. He was gone.
We ran up on the trail and found a bloodied sandal and a
hat and a 1936 French Mauser.

As things quieted down it was revealed that the
man who had been under guard had bolted at the first
shot. His guard shot him as he tried to escape. He lay
moaning for a few minutes and died.

Somehow action and death act as a ghastly tonic
for men. Everyone was joking and laughing to hide their
excitement and fear.

Many men went and examined the body. Dead people fascinate men.

The rest of the column moved up and we set up a defensive perimeter. It was noon and it was decided to eat.

"Yeah, one of the bastards got away, but we hit him," said one of the "heroes" to one of the men who had been further back. "There's a blood trail. Look at this mauser, will ya? Beaut, ain't it?"

"Boy, this one's sure fucked up, isn't he? Who got him?"

A GI with a huge knife in his hand: "Shit! He doesn't even have enough hair to cut a tassel with. What'll I do?"

"Cut off the cocksucker's ear."

Later I saw the man decapitated. His head rested on the ground, with one eye closed and one eye open, forming a horrible wink. A lit cigarette burned between his graying lips. The gory corpse, headless and bloody, lay several feet away. Men are savages.

Several women and small children crouched together next to a hut as we ate our C rats. An old man, a husband to one of the women, was inside the hut being questioned. He was being kicked, also, and he began crying and screaming. His graying wife, blind and holding a cane, was bawling. The kids had quieted down; the shooting had terrified them, and their faces were stained with dried up tears.

Some soldiers chased chickens around, who squawked wildly as they fled.

Chapter VIII.
October 8, 1967

The jaded man stumbles again;
for the last time.
He tries with all his strength
to regain his feet,
But his muscles are all played
out with past efforts,
He dies struggling to stand
once more,
He dies grimacing with trial
But struggling also with a faint,
sweet smile,
For he knows he has lived.

October 8, 1967

WESTERN UNION
TELEGRAM

W. P. MARSHALL
CHAIRMAN OF THE BOARD

R. W. McFALL
PRESIDENT

1967 OCT 10 PM 2 55

The filing time shown in the date line on domestic telegrams is LOCAL TIME at point of origin. Time of receipt is LOCAL TIME at point of destination

SF427 (31)SYB201   ML-STL

SY WB137 XV GOVT PD WASHINGTON DC 10 545PEDT

MR AND MRS FRANK E CHRISTOFERSON, DONT DLR BTWN 10PM AND 6
AM DONT PHONE

3 THORNDELL DRIVE STL

THE SECRETARY OF THE ARMY HAS ASKED ME TO EXPRESS HIS DEEP
REGRET THAT YOUR SON SPECIALIST SCOTT A CHRISTOFERSON HAS
BEEN MISSING IN VIETNAM SINCE 8 OCT 67. HE WAS LAST SEEN ON
COMBAT OPERATION WHEN ENGAGED HOSTILE FORCE IN FIREFIGHT.
SEARCH IS IN PROGRESS.

YOU WILL BE ADVISED PROMPTLY WHEN FURTHER INFORMATION IS
RECEIVED. IN ORDER TO PROTECT ANY INFORMATION THAT MIGHT BE
USED TO YOUR SONS DETRIMENT YOUR COOPERATION IS REQUESTED IN
MAKING PUBLIC ONLY INFORMATION CONCERNING HIS NAME, RANK SERVICE
NUMBER AND DATE OF BIRTH. THIS CONFIRMS PERSONAL
NOTIFICATION MADE BY A REPRESENTATIVE OF THE SECRETARY OF THE

WESTERN UNION
TELEGRAM

W. P. MARSHALL
CHAIRMAN OF THE BOARD

R. W. McFALL
PRESIDENT

The filing time shown in the date line on domestic telegrams is LOCAL TIME at point of origin. Time of receipt is LOCAL TIME at point of destination

ARMY

KENNETH G WICKHAM MAJ GENL USA OF THE ADJT GENL.

Your Hero and Mine, Scott

From *The Screaming Eagle, November, 1967*

60 NVA Killed In Battle

Chu-Lai A company of the 101st Airborne fought off two well-armed North Vietnamese Army companies northwest of here recently, killing a confirmed 60 NVA in a four and a half hour battle fought during heavy monsoon rains.

A Co. of the 2nd Bn (Abn) 327th Inf. reported the high enemy body count while suffering 17 paratroopers killed and four wounded.

The "No Slack" paratroopers were sweeping a valley 18 miles west of Tam Ky when at 1:40 p.m. they received 82 mm mortar fire. The enemy mortars wounded several Screaming Eagles. Following the mortar attack, the NVA force initiated a two-prong assault cutting off and encircling one paratrooper platoon. Other elements of the Screaming Eagle company had to break through the enemy ranks in bloody, hand-to-hand fighting.

Medevac helicopter pilots braved heavy rains and zero visibility weather to evacuate seriously wounded paratroopers. Those with minor wounds refused evacuation.

Air Force jets and helicopter gun-
ships were grounded as the rains grew
heavier. Artillery support had to cut
off to avoid hitting paratroopers
when the fighting was closest.

B Co. and the nearby Hawk reconnaissance platoon moved toward the be-
sieged A Co. Enroute, B Co. killed
three NVA in green camouflaged uniforms at 3:15 p.m.

Capt John Lawton, Bethesda, MD, commander of A Co., was hit during the
contact yet directed the paratroopers
with wounds in the leg and shoulders
while lying on the ground.

His radio-telephone operator and the
artillery forward observer were hit
as they ran to his aid.

Also killed in the contact was a combat reporter from the brigade information office. He was hit by enemy
fire while firing on advancing enemy—
the fourth information specialist to
die in battle since the brigade arrived in Vietnam.

The battle ended at 5:30 p.m. Twenty
one individual weapons were captured.
A Russian light machine gun, a 60 mm
mortar sigh and assorted rockets also
were found.

Five Viet Cong were killed in other contacts, bringing the day's body count to 68. The 68 kills made Operation Wheeler the largest single sweep conducted by the Screaming Eagles since their arrival in Vietnam July 29, 1965.

Chapter IX.
In Memoriam

29 October 1967

Dear Mr. and Mrs. Christofferson:

We want you to know how deeply we share your sorrow in the loss of your son and our very good friend.

We remember the day when he first came to work for us. Christofferson wasn't easy for all of us to remember. It often came out Christopherson. After a couple of weeks, everybody started calling him "Chris." I guess he went along with the nickname because he would call in and say, "...tell 'em Chris said so-and-so..." or he would write Chris on the top of his copy when he submitted it for editing.

Whatever the nickname, Chris was liked by everyone. His enthusiasm and good humor was contagious. He could make you laugh in spite of yourself. And he was never discouraged by anything. No matter how hard it rained or when the Cards lost a few games at the beginning of the season, Chris was always optimistic.

We have an expression over here about the fellow who always takes care of his job and is never out of line: "Straight-arrow," they say. That was Chris.

When Chris had a slight bout with malaria, he was disgusted. He came in saying, "They tell me I've got malaria. That's crazy." Over his objections, he went to Qui Nhon for hospitalization. He didn't like it. Soon he was out and came bouncing in the shop saying: "Boy, it's sure good to get out of the

168

hospital. You know, they were getting ready to put me on KP? I told them if I was that well I was going back to the brigade."

That was the happy-go-lucky side of Chris all of us knew and loved.

He loved baseball, too. When the Cards had clinched the race, Chris really razzed the fans of other clubs. When Lt. Hana, the assistant information officer, wrote the story which went with the picture printed in the Globe and Post Dispatch, Chris helped find the fellows from St. Louis serving here. The story was written in September. Chris read it before it was mailed to the newspaper. The little Vietnamese boy who appeared in the picture was a lad Chris found in our area and talked him into putting on the T-shirt. It was a fun day when the Card fans posed for the picture.

Chris talked a lot of baseball in the field, too. As a combat correspondent, Chris would visit various companies of the 2nd Battalion (Airborne), 327th Infantry, one of four infantry battalions with his brigade. He covered his battalion newsbeat with efficiency and his good humor. Usually, he would be out two or three days, then he would come back and write his stories. He would remain here in our forward base camp for three or four days and then return to his battalion news beat, searching for stories about the paratrooper at war. He liked being in the field with the troops and would grow restless when he wasn't with them.

On Saturday, October 7th, Chris caught a ride on a helicopter and went back to the battalion where he teamed up with Company A. Chris had been with Company B the time before and, like all of our combat correspondents and photographers, Chris rotated around, insuring each company got equal coverage in our news releases.

Saturday night, the fringe of Typhoon Carla triggered a monsoon storm here. It poured down Saturday night and all day Sunday.

Chris was moving with the 2nd platoon on Sunday afternoon. They were moving through a valley, investigating abandoned huts. Nothing of any consequence turned up during the search and the platoon then moved over to a sort of thicket with scrubby trees, vines and underbrush. The platoon searched the thicket without incident. At the end of the thicket was an open rice paddy bordered on four sides by clumps of trees.

The platoon moved out of the thicket, along a rice paddy dike and crossed the corner of the paddy. As they entered the treeline on their left, the enemy opened fire. Everyone began firing back and took up defensive cover in the treeline.

The rest of the company—about 500 yards to the rear of the platoon—moved to join them. They too came under fire as they maneuvered toward the 2nd platoon.

Moments later, the 2nd platoon was attacked by an estimated North Vietnamese Army company—about 200 enemy. Every paratrooper fired his weapon and laid down a withering volume of fire. Enemy dead fell everywhere as they pressed the attack on the defending platoon.

Other Americans joined the battle and drove off the enemy. Sixty enemy were dead; 17 Americans. Enemy bodies were scattered around Chris' position. He made them pay heavily for his life. He acquitted himself in the highest tradition.

Chris used to sit around and talk with us about his Dad. He told us about his father winning a Silver Star while flying off the USS Hornet. In Chris' judgment, his Dad was a hero without equal.

I am enclosing copies of a picture taken by one of Chris' buddies in the afternoon of September 27th as he sat writing here in our office. We like this picture very much because it shows him and the personality we loved so much.

You will also find three contact sheets of pictures Chris took one afternoon when he and a buddy went down to the beach to relax. If you wish, we can furnish you larger prints of any picture on the sheets or send the negatives to you.

Capt. John Miller received a letter from Chris' sister requesting a copy of the picture which appeared in the newspaper with the Cardinal story. We have ordered extra copies of the picture and will forward them to you later.

I hope our words about Chris—the Chris we knew and loved—comfort you. He will always be held in warmest affection by all of us in the information office. He was "Straight Arrow."

Sincerely,
Billy E. Spangler
Major, Infantry
Information Officer

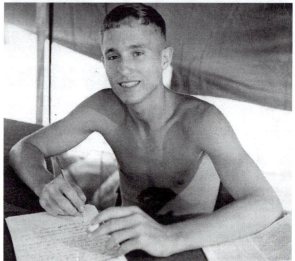

172

These pictures were provided to the Christofferson family by the Public Information Office after Scott's death. **Left,** *above, Scott (on right) interviews another soldier; Left, below, Scott at work on a story;* **Above,** *Scott with other Cardinal Baseball fans posing with a Vietnamese boy for a public relations piece for the St. Louis Post-Dispatch*

HEADQUARTERS
AMERICAL DIVISION
APO San Francisco 96374

GENERAL ORDERS
NUMBER 1512

2 December 1967

AWARD OF THE SILVER STAR

1. TC 320. The following AWARD is announced posthumously.

CHRISTOFFERSON, SCOTT A. RA 17 729 663, SPECIALIST FOUR E4, United States Army, Headquarters and Headquarters Company, 1st Brigade, 101st Airborne Division APO 96347
Awarded: Silver Star
Date action: 8 October 1967
Theater: Republic of Vietnam
Reason: For gallantry in action against a hostile force on 8 October 1967 in the Republic of Vietnam. Specialist Four Christofferson distinguished himself by his fearless courage and intense devotion to duty. On that date, his platoon was attacked by two North Vietnamese Army Companies using automatic weapons, mortars and recoilless rifles. When ordered to withdraw, Specialist Christofferson elected to remain in his vulnerable position to cover the withdrawl of his comrades. Despite heavy mortar and automatic weapons fire, Specialist Christofferson was unrelenting in his resistance of the enemy until fatally wounded. Due directly to his gallant efforts, many of his comrades were able to reach safety. Specialist Four Christofferson's undaunted determination and unselfish concern for the lives of his fellow soldiers were in keeping with the finest traditions of the military service and reflect great credit upon himself, the Americal Division and the United States Army.
Authority: By direction of the President under the provisions of the Act of Congress, approved 9 July 1918.

FOR THE COMMANDER:

OFFICIAL:

ROBERT H. MUSSER
Colonel, GS
Chief of Staff

DONALD Y. B. CHUNG
LTC, AGC
Adjutant General

Epilogue
Three Thorndell

It was early in the Spring of 1968 in St. Louis. Frank and Barbara Christofferson chatted companionably in the kitchen of their home at Three Thorndell Drive in the suburb of Richmond Heights, on a March weekday evening after Frank had arrived home from a long day at the office. Frank's mood was reflective. The couple had been married for 25 years, since December of 1942 when they joined hands in front of a Roman Catholic priest in a hurriedly-arranged ceremony before Frank shipped out to the South Pacific, where he was to fly missions from a Naval aircraft carrier. They had weathered the War, several cross-country moves, the births of their eight children, an assortment of garden-variety ups and downs with their marriage and family, and, in October 1967, the death in Vietnam of their nineteen-year-old son, Scott.

Frank mused that their lives were much calmer and more stable now than they had been at times in the past. Their marriage was strong. He spoke hopefully about the state of the project at work; he was Director of Flight for McDonnell-Douglas Aircraft Corporation, and had been involved for several years in the development of a much-lauded aircraft collision avoidance system. He noted that his older children were doing well; oldest son, Clyde, 24, was a successful law student and daughter, Jan, 22, had recently joined the American Red Cross in a paid staff position. The younger five children, three boys and two girls, ages 13 to 7, were doing fine and at present, no one was causing undue parental concern.

In short, he said, he felt good about the state of his life, work, family and marriage. He paused, and added wistfully, "I'd sure like to be able to talk to Scott."

Just a few days later, on St. Patrick's Day, Frank worked late, and had to miss the father-daughter square dance at his twelve-year-old daughter, Carrie's elementary school. Carrie attended alone, and her school principal filled in for Frank, much to Carrie's pre-adolescent dismay. Frank swung by the school on his way home to pick her up when it was over. Rubbing the back of his head with one hand as he steered the station wagon with the other, he commented absently that he had had a bad headache all evening.

Later, after he and Barbara had retired to bed for the night, Frank rolled over, flung an arm over his wife and whispered haltingly, "I'm...going...." before lapsing into a coma from which he never recovered. Frank suffered a ruptured cerebral aneurysm, and spent 10 days in a coma before he died on March 27, 1968. He was 49.

Family lore has it that he died of a broken heart.

Above, clockwise: Frank E. Christofferson accepts a posthumous medal on behalf of his son, Scott; Scott with older sister, Jan, prior to shipping out to Vietnam in May, 1967; a family photo c. 1963 of (clockwise) Clyde, Scott, Carl, Frank C., Jim, and Frank E. **At left:** The family of Carl F. Meier, a high school classmate of Scott's who also was killed in Vietnam, established the memorial pictured here, which is located in a place of honor on the Ladue Horton Watkins High School grounds in Ladue, Missouri.

177

Tuned In on Baseball

Six St. Louis area paratroopers with the First Brigade, 101st Airborne Division, are joined by 15-year-old Xuan, a resident of Chu Lai, Vietnam, in wishing the Cardinals luck in the World Series. Front row, from left: Pfc. Robert J. Saddler, 2831 Dayton, St. Louis; Xuan; Spec. 4 Scott Christofferson, 3 Thorndell, Rich-

mond Heights. Back row—Capt. John E. Miller, 2005 South Roanoke, Springfield, Mo.; Spec. 4 Edward W. Eppy, 1104 Purtscher drive, Peoria, Ill.; Staff Sgt. Lester E. Hite, 4204 Miniel court, St. Louis, and Capt. Michael Welch, 1111 Dawn drive, Belleville.

The newspaper clipping pictured above appeared in the St. Louis Post-Dispatch on October 8, 1967, the day Scott was killed in action in Vietnam. His family was notified of his death October 10.

Made in the USA